MAURETANIA

TRIUMPH
AND
RESURRECTION

Charles Pears' painting of *Mauretania* passing under the Forth Bridge at the end of her final voyage was commissioned for the Tourist Class Smoking Room on *Queen Mary*.
[Peter Newall Collection]

MAURETANIA

TRIUMPH AND RESURRECTION

PETER NEWALL

Ships in Focus Publications
Published in the UK in 2006 by Ships in Focus Publications,
18 Franklands, Longton
Preston PR4 5PD

Printed by Amadeus Press Ltd., Cleckheaton
ISBN 1 901703 53 3

Cover design by Steve Waddington, Amadeus Press.

Above: *Mauretania* at speed after 1924. *[Ambrose Greenway Collection]*

This book is dedicated to Harold Peto, whose legacy lives on in his wonderful gardens and designs for Mauretania

Mauretania 1927. *[Zogolovitch Collection]*

CONTENTS

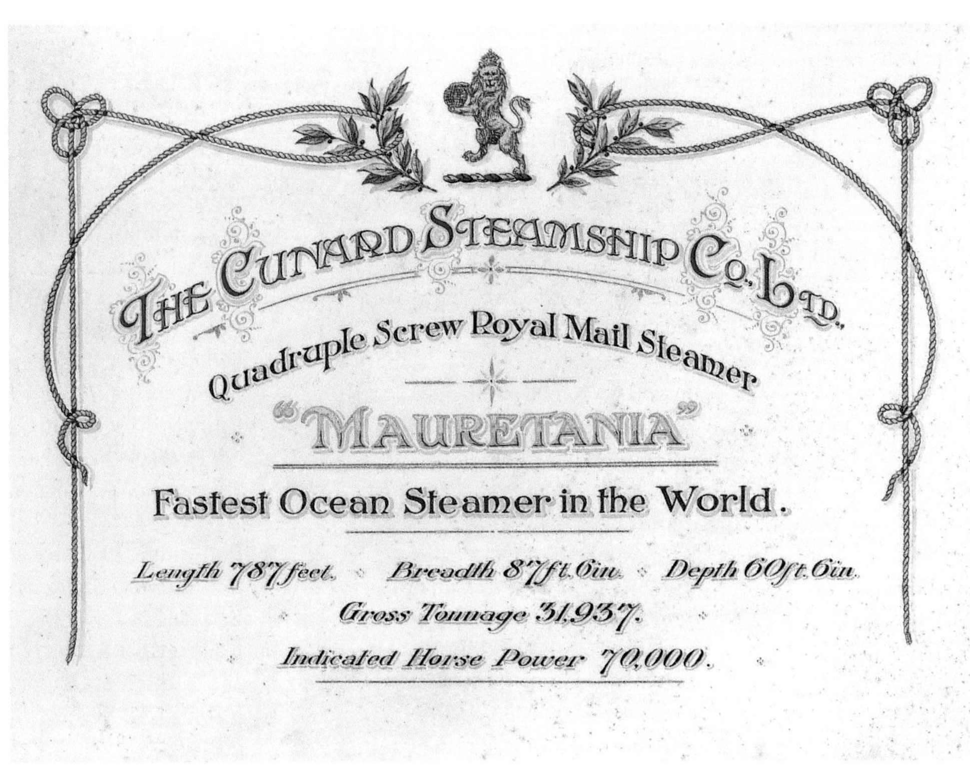

Mauretania 1907. *[Zogolovitch Collection]*

INTRODUCTION

One hundred years after she was completed, *Mauretania* remains one of the most famous liners ever built. A lucky ship, she held the transatlantic Blue Riband record for 22 years. Despite her being scrapped in 1936, many of her magnificent interiors are still scattered around England. In fact, no other demolished liner of the past has so much material still on view. This was the main reason for starting an enjoyable and fascinating voyage of discovery in search of *Mauretania* and her remains. It was also apparent that, despite her fame, there has been relatively little written about *Mauretania* and her career.

Although many *Mauretania* items have been unearthed during this quest, there are probably many more which, for one reason or another, have lost their association with the great liner. It is hoped that this book will assist in finding and preserving these pieces for posterity.

I would like to offer a great 'thank you' to the following people and organisations who have either given me unrestricted access to *Mauretania* items or have shared information and provided images. Without their generous support and co-operation, this book would not have been possible. If I have left anyone out, please accept my sincere apologies:

Daniel Albert, Alastair Arnott, Sarah and John Avery, Carolyn Ball, Declan Barriskill, Ruth Barriskill, Andrew Bell, Julian Bell, Peter Belloc, Diane Bilbey, Steve Booth, Colin Boyd, Bob Bradshaw, Ian Buxton, Stephen Card, Elizabeth Cartwright-Hignett, Andrew Clark, Howard Colton, Kay and Roy Cope, Luis Miguel Correia, Peter Cullen, Charlie Dragonette, Jennifer Dunn, Peter Eatenton, Maurizio Eliseo, Ian Farquhar, Suzanne Fisher, Lindsay Ford, Peter Fuller, Jez Gale, Michael Gallagher, Adam Gratwick, David Green, Ambrose Greenway, Valerie Hart, Keith Hatchard, Fred Hawks, Gordon Hawksley, David.Hollingworth, Roland Humble, Keith Hutchinson, Paul F. Johnston, Martin Lambert, Susan Lines, Paul Linfield, Paul Louden-Brown, Eleanor Moffat, Greta Morley, Judy Newall, Michael Pocock, Liz Quick, Ian Rae, Alun Roberts, Ann Runeckles, Ken Saunders, George Scott, Garry Shutlak, Tony Smith, Charlotte Swire, Howard Turner, David Watkins, Robin Whalley, Ian Whitehead, Carola and Roger Zogolovitch.

British American Tobacco, Bristol City Library, Cunard Line, Deva Antiques, The Discovery Museum, Dorking Advertiser, Flybe., Guildhall Library, Henry Boot PLC, Iford Manor, Imperial War Museum, Leatherhead Museum, Merseyside Maritime Museum, National Archives, National Maritime Museum, Nova Scotia Archives and Records Management, Ocean Liner Auctions, Pinewood Studios Ltd., pml Signs, Poole Museum Services, Science Museum, Smithsonian Institution, Southampton Library, Southampton Maritime Museum, Southern Daily Echo, Tayler & Fletcher, Taunton's College, Tyne and Wear Archives, University of Liverpool, Special Collections & Archives, University of Newcastle upon Tyne, Victoria and Albert Museum, World Ship Society.

Special thanks also to Lisa Royall who helped with much of the proof reading and to Robert Shopland, former editor of 'Ships Monthly', whose fond memories of The Mauretania, Bristol inspired this fascinating story.

My publishers have again been a joy to work with and I thank them for their support in getting this project finalised.

Peter Newall,
Blandford Forum
September 2006

SOURCES

Primary sources

Cunard Line archives, University of Liverpool
Cunard Magazine
Engineering magazine *Mauretania* special edition 1907
Fairplay
Hampton & Sons May 1935 *Mauretania* auction catalogue (annotated)
Lloyd's List
Lloyd's Weekly Shipping Index
Metal Industries Limited archives, University of Newcastle upon Tyne
National Archives, *Mauretania* logbooks BT100 series
Poole Council minute books
Shipbuilding and Shipping Record
The Shipbuilder
*The Shipbuilder Mauretania s*pecial edition 1907
Southern Daily Echo
Swan Hunter archives, Tyne and Wear Archives
The Mauretania Syndicate catalogue
World War One Service List

Other souces

Aylmer, Gerald, *RMS Mauretania The Ship and her Record*, Percival Marshall, 1933 or 1934
Bisset, Sir James, *My Early Years in Steamers*, Angus and Robertson, 1960
Bonsor, N., *North Atlantic Seaway*, Brookside Publications, 1975
Buxton, Ian, *Mauretania and Her Builders*, 'Mariners Mirror', Volume 82 , 1996, Number 1
Buxton, Ian, *Metal Industries, Shipbreaking at Rosyth and Charlestown*, World Ship Society, 1992
Cartwright-Hignett, Elizabeth, *The Peto Garden at Iford Manor*, 1999
Hatchard, Keith, unpublished manuscript about life at the Boat House in the 1930s and 1940s.Hyde, F.E., *Cunard and the North Atlantic*, Macmillan Press, 1975
Jordan, Humfrey, *Mauretania Landfalls and Departures of Twenty-five Years*, Hodder and Stoughton, 1936
Longbottom, Ken, *Liverpool and the Mersey, Volume 1: Gladstone Dock and the Great Liners*, Silver Link Publishing, 1995
Moody, Burt, *150 Years of Southampton Docks*, Kingfisher Railway Productions, 1988
Owen, Gareth and Burford, Brian, *The Pinewood Story*, Reynolds & Hearn, 2000
Plumridge, Lt-Colonel John, *Hospital Ships and Ambulance Trains*, Seeley, Service & Co., 1975
Rostron, Sir Arthur, *Home From the Sea*, Cassell & Company Ltd., 1931
Rutherford, W., *The Man Who Built the Mauretania*, Hillside Press, 1934
Smith, Ken, *Mauretania Pride of the Tyne*, Newcastle Libraries, 1997
Whale, Derek, *The Liners of Liverpool, Part 1*, Countyvise Limited, 1986
Wilkinson, Max, *The Demolition of the Mauretania*, The Manchester Association of Engineers, 1940

PART ONE

TRIUMPH

MAURETANIA'S CAREER

Concept, design and construction 1902-1907

On 26th June 1897, *Lucania* (12,952/1893), Cunard Line's transatlantic record breaker and the world's largest ship, took part in the Diamond Jubilee fleet review at Spithead, the stretch of water between Portsmouth and the Isle of Wight. This grand occasion was held to celebrate the sixtieth year of Queen Victoria's reign. During her long sovereignty, not only had Britain's navy conquered the waves, its empire had also grown into the largest in history, encompassing about a quarter of the earth's population.

At the time, it was claimed that the Spithead Fleet Review was the largest ensemble of warships anchored in one place. As Edward Prince of Wales, aboard the Royal Yacht *Victoria and Albert*, led the way through the fleet, the occasion was interrupted by the spectacle of a small vessel dashing at over 30 knots through the line of ships. In one fell swoop Charles Parson's *Turbinia* demonstrated to the world the superiority of his new turbine-driven marine engine.

Also in 1897, Sir John Burns (1829-1901), son of one of the founders of Cunard Line, was given a peerage and became the first Lord Inverclyde. Later that year Cunard lost the title of owning the largest ship in the world and the distinguished Blue Riband for the fastest Atlantic crossing to the new 14,349-ton German liner *Kaiser Wilhelm der Grosse*. This was a major blow for a company which considered itself as the premier transatlantic line. Cunard's prestige was further dented two years later when its main rival at Liverpool, White Star Line, took delivery of the 17,274-ton *Oceanic*, the largest liner in the world. She was followed in 1901 by *Celtic,* the first of a quartet of White Star liners over 20,000-tons. Cunard's express liners of the early 1890s, *Lucania* and *Campania*, were now outdated and the Cunard board started to discuss building new fast steamers for the Liverpool-New York service. The Chairman of Cunard Line at the time was Sir George Arbuthnot Burns, the second Lord Inverclyde.

Lord Inverclyde, instigator of the project.
[Zogolovitch Collection]

In 1902 the Cunard technical department produced specifications for two 700-feet-long ships able to carry 2,000 passengers and capable of speeds of 23-24 knots. They would be about the same size as White Star Line's big ships and as fast as the current German record holder, *Deutschland.* Meanwhile, in April 1902 John Pierpoint Morgan (1837-1913), the American financier and banker, announced the formation of the International Mercantile Marine Corporation of New Jersey. This company was created to take over a number of key transatlantic lines including White Star Line. This threatened not only Cunard Line's position across the Atlantic but also the independence of British shipping on this key trade route. Urgent talks took place with the British Government and on 30th September 1902, the then Prime Minister Arthur Balfour announced that Cunard had been given a low interest loan to build two new ships. The company would also receive a generous annual operating subsidy as these liners would be designed for use as armed merchant cruisers by the Admiralty in times of war. A key condition of the agreement was that Cunard Line remained in British ownership.

Mr. G. B. Hunter
[Zogolovitch Collection]

In October 1902 four shipyards, two Scottish and two English, were asked to tender for the new liners. Each ship was to be powered by reciprocating engines despite a proposal from Charles Parsons for turbine engines to be considered. The yards approached were John Brown and Co. Ltd., Clydebank, Fairfield Shipbuilding and Engineering Co. Ltd., Govan, Vickers Sons and Maxim Ltd., Barrow-in-Furness and the Newcastle yard of C. S. Swan, Hunter Ltd., Wallsend. Despite being the smallest of the companies, Swan Hunter was added to the list because of its proposal to expand the yard should it win the bid. The company was also building Cunard's 13,603-ton *Carpathia*. The chairman G. B. Hunter started merger discussions with the nearby shipyard Wigham Richardson and Co. Ltd. He also approached the engine builder Wallsend Slipway and Engineering Co. Ltd., which was run by Andrew Laing. Laing had previously worked for Fairfields and was responsible for *Campania*'s engine design.

Tests were undertaken by the Admiralty at its Experimental Works in Haslar, near Gosport, to ascertain the optimum dimensions for a ship capable of doing 25 knots and with a draught to be able to enter the ports of New York and Liverpool. The findings released in February 1903 proposed a length of 760 feet and a breadth of 85 feet. These increased dimensions created logistical problems for both Fairfield Shipbuilding and Engineering and Vickers Sons and Maxim. They dropped out of contention leaving John Brown and Swan Hunter to be told on 8th May 1903 that 'the Directors were inclined to favourably consider the placing of an order with each of them for one of the proposed fast steamers'. This gave the green light for the proposed merger between C. S. Swan, Hunter Ltd. and Wigham Richardson and Co. Ltd., which was agreed on 26th May. The following month the new company was registered as Swan, Hunter and Wigham Richardson Ltd. Earlier that year, Swan, Hunter had also obtained a controlling interest in the Wallsend Slipway and Engineering Company.

In July 1903 Cunard Line agreed the terms of its Government loan of £2.6 million at 2.75% interest to be paid back over twenty years. Revised specifications, still with reciprocating engines, were also sent to John Brown and Swan, Hunter and Wigham Richardson. However, in August another approach was made by the Parson Marine Steam Turbine Company and, possibly due to pressure from the Admiralty, Cunard decided to reconsider the possibility of turbine power. A committee was set up and on 25th February 1904 it recommended to the Cunard Line board that turbine machinery should be used for both ships. This bold move meant further tests and design changes and in July the two builders submitted plans for quadruple-screw, turbine-driven ships, each with a length of 760 feet and a breadth of 87.5 feet. The proposed tonnage of over 30,000 also ensured that when they entered service they would be, by a large margin, the world's largest ships. They were also the first transatlantic liners to be fitted with four propellers.

William Watson, Cunard Chairman, 1905 to 1909. *[Zogolovitch Collection]*

The keels for the as yet unnamed new ships were laid a day apart. The keel for Hull No. 367 was laid at Clydebank on 17th August 1904 whilst that for Hull No. 735 was laid at Wallsend the following day. Since October 1903, Swan, Hunter and Wigham Richardson had invested heavily in modernising the yard and its facilities. This included two huge covered building berths, new steelworking shops and a new 140-ton floating crane for the installation of the machinery. A self-propelled 47.5-foot scale model of the hull was built at Wallsend and tested extensively in the Northumberland Dock. It was used not only to test wind resistance but, more importantly, to establish the most suitable set-up for the four propellers.

Work on the new liner was well underway at Wallsend whilst the details of the ship were still being hammered out between the Admiralty, Cunard and the builders. The final contract with Swan, Hunter and Wigham Richardson was signed on 18th May 1905. Meanwhile, Cunard had commenced its search for a designer for the main public rooms. After protracted negotiations, the architect Harold Peto was appointed the interior designer for Hull No. 735 on 13th September 1905. A detailed account of Harold Peto's appointment and a description of the interiors can be found on pages 46 to 47 and 48 to 68 respectively.

The question of names for the two ships had still to be resolved, despite a request by the Admiralty in November 1904 to make a decision. Three pairs of names were considered: *Albania* and *Moravia*; *Britannia* and *Hesperia* and *Britannia* and *Hibernia*. In the end, at a board meeting on 15th February 1906, it was agreed that the names would be *Lusitania* for Hull No. 367 and *Mauritania* for Hull No. 735. Three months later the spelling of *Mauritania* was changed to *Mauretania*. Lusitania was the Roman province on the Iberian Peninsula, which included modern-day Portugal and much of western Spain. Mauretania was a Roman province in North Africa. The Roman connection was particularly pertinent for the Wallsend shipyard as it was situated at the end of the 73-mile long Hadrian's Wall, which was built by the Romans as protection from the Scottish tribes to the north. Sadly, Lord Inverclyde, the instigator of the grand plan, did not live to see the completion of his two super liners. He died on the 8th October 1905, aged only 44, and was succeeded as chairman by William Watson.

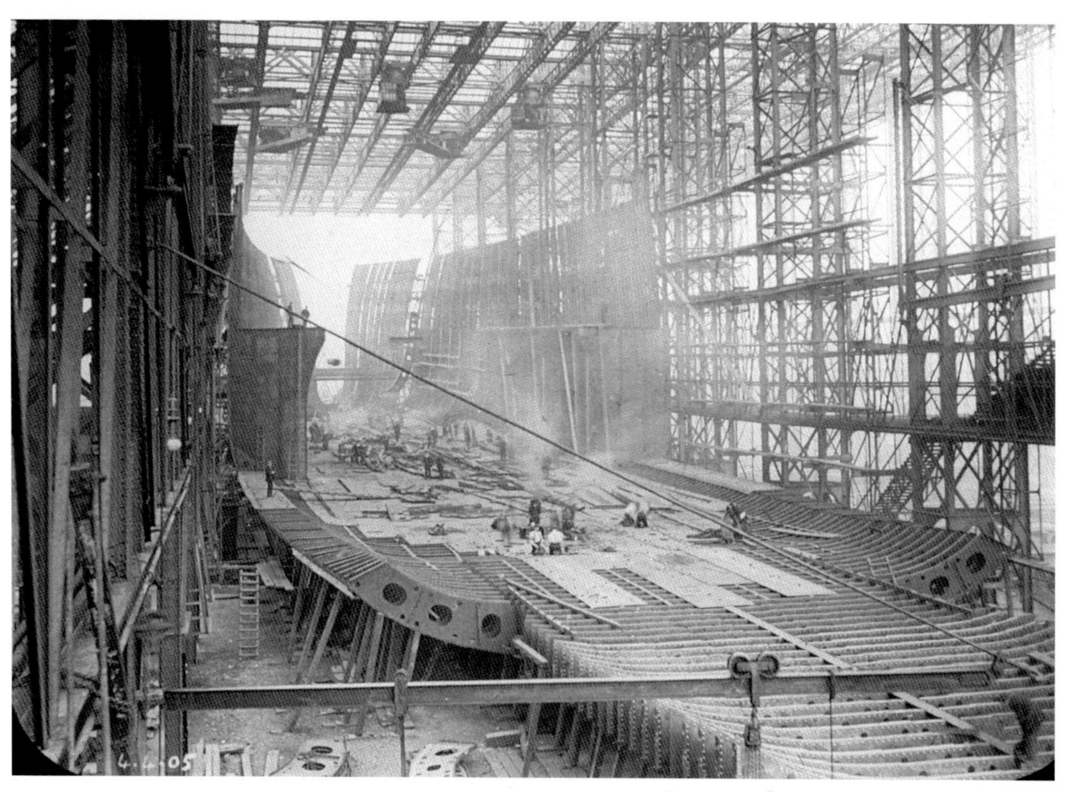

Mauretania was built in a huge glass-roofed shed with travelling overhead cranes. When work commenced, because the layout of the turbine machinery had yet to be finalised, the fore end framing was completed first. This was the scene in early 1905. *[Tyne and Wear Archives]*

Mauretania's immense hull took almost two years to complete. Because the details of her turbine engines and their fittings were only finalised after construction had started, the work was concentrated initially on the midships and forward end of the ship. Her possible role as an armed merchant cruiser meant a requirement from the Admiralty that all her vital machinery and equipment be situated below the waterline. At the time, gunfire was the most likely form of attack, but during the First World War this changed with the use of submarines and torpedoes. Described as 'practically unsinkable', *Mauretania* had 175 separate watertight compartments whilst the four boiler rooms were protected by coal bunkers which ran fore and aft on either side of the hull. The balanced rudder and steering gear were also situated beneath the waterline. In the event of war, she would be fitted with twelve six-inch guns, four on the fore deck and the rest on the shelter deck, amidships and aft.

On 7th September 1906 construction on the slipway was complete and *Mauretania* was prepared for her launch on the 20th September. Whilst she featured the Cunard white hull band above red boot-topping (i.e. the area below and just above the waterline), her hull was painted grey with white upperworks. This was done to show off her lines to best effect on launch day. Despite work starting a day apart, *Lusitania* had been launched at Clydebank three months earlier on 7th June. Because of the sheer scale of the work involved, the May 1905 contract between Cunard and Swan, Hunter and Wigham Richardson specified that the ship would be ready for handover in thirty months, i.e. in November 1907. With fourteen months left to finish the job, the shipyard was confident that she would be delivered on time. Cunard Line had originally hoped that Queen Alexandra could have launched the ship to coincide with her July visit to Newcastle with King Edward VII.

On the day of the launch guests were treated to a carefully staged tour of the machinery in the fitting out yard, a little way down river from the slipway. This was designed to show off the immense size of the equipment, with cars driving through the funnels and between the boilers. The actual launch took place soon after 4.15pm on 20th September. The ceremony was performed by Winston Churchill's aunt, the Dowager Duchess of Roxburghe (1854-1923), who had been Mistress of the Robes to Queen Victoria and was also the sister-in-law of the First Lord of the Admiralty, Lord Tweedmouth. In little over a minute the vessel was in the river, held in place by a series of chains attached to the hull. Tugs then moved her to the fitting-out berth, which was made up of two large dolphins (mooring posts), with a connecting bridge to the shoreline.

Over the next twelve months the ship was fitted out with machinery, funnels, masts, equipment and interiors. Much of the material was loaded aboard by *Titan*, the giant floating crane, one of the largest in the world, which had been specially built in Germany. The boilers were installed during 1906 and the four boiler rooms occupied most of the machinery space. In total there were 23 double-ended boilers, two single-ended boilers and 192 furnaces. The fires were stoked by 204 firemen. They were divided into three four-hour watches, with the job of bringing the coal to the furnaces done by 120

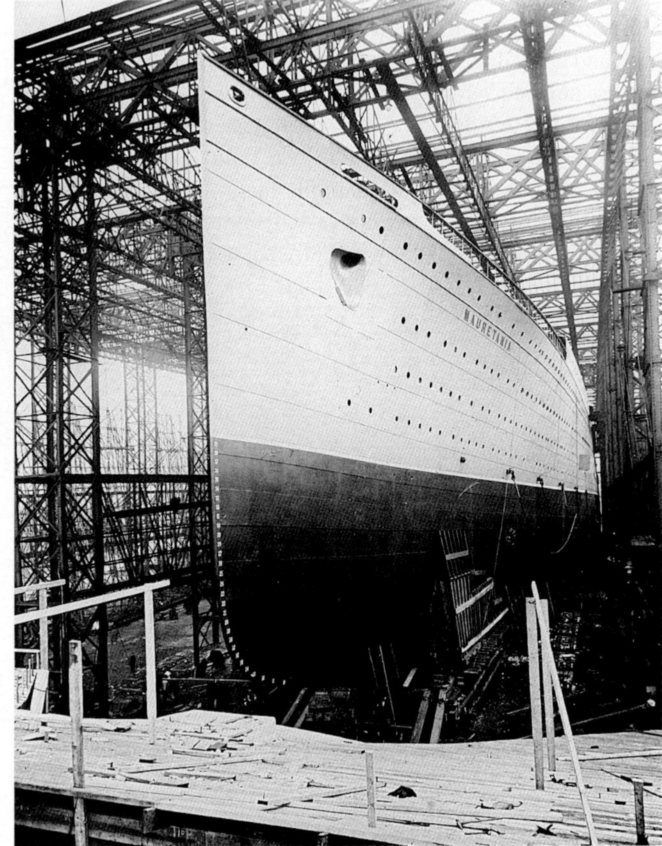

Contruction progressed until September 1906 when the hull was ready for launching. The scaffolding was removed and a wooden platform for the launch ceremony was constructed. Her hull was painted grey as this highlighted her knife-like stem, curved stern and fine lines to best effect. *[Left: Ian Rae Collection, above and top right opposite: Zogolovitch Collection]*

trimmers. This backbreaking work was undertaken in extreme heat and was conducted with great skill. With a daily consumption of up to 900 tons of coal, the huge amount of ash generated was removed by specially designed ash hoists, mixed with water and pumped well clear of the ship's side. Exhaust fumes were also discharged through the four large, raked funnels, one for each boiler room. To improve the performance of the boilers, 32 electrically driven fans provided a forced draught, which also helped reduce the temperature in the engine room.

The steam from the boilers was used to drive the turbines with their thousands of individually-made blades. Two high-pressure ahead turbines were connected directly to the outer wing shafts and propellers whilst two low-pressure ahead turbines and two astern turbines were connected to the two centre shafts and propellers. To give some idea of the immense power produced by the engine rooms of the two sisters, it was claimed that the total output (68,000 indicated horse-power) was 75 percent greater than any other machinery installed aboard a passenger ship. When she was completed in September 1907, *Mauretania*'s gross tonnage was 31,938. As this was 1,116 tons greater than *Lusitania*, she became the world's largest ship. She also cost more to build (£1.812 million) than her sister (£1.625 million).

With a crew of 938 and a passenger capacity of 2,176 (563 first class, 475 second class and 1,138 third class), her dimensions were: overall length 790 feet; length between perpendiculars 760 feet and draught 36 feet 2 inches.

The launch ceremony was performed by the Dowager Duchess of Roxburghe on Thursday, 20th September 1906. The attendees at the launch were dwarfed by the enormous size of *Mauretania*. *[Tyne & Wear Archives]*

Cunard "S.S. Mauretania"

Builders Swan Hunter & Wigham Richardson Ltd

The Chairman & Directors of
Swan Hunter & Wigham Richardson Ltd
Wallsend on Tyne,
request the honour of the Company of

at the Launch of the Cunard Steamship Company's
Quadruple Turbine Steamship
"Mauretania"
on Thursday September 20th 1906 at 3.30 P.M.

The Naming Ceremony
will be performed by Her Grace
The Dowager Duchess of Roxburghe.

R.S.V.P.

Mauretania was launched soon after 4.15pm and entered the water in just over a minute. Even with the removal of the landing stage on the opposite side of the River Tyne, the amount of clearance was very small and allowed no room for error. *[Top and middle right: Zogolovitch Collection; middle left: George Scott Collection; bottom: Peter Newall Collection]*

The fitting out took almost a year. Much of the heavy machinery was lifted aboard by *Titan*, one of the world's largest floating cranes. Here the last of the 25 boilers is being lowered into place at the end of 1906. *[Bob Bradshaw Collection]*

These two photos show her nearly finished. The ship being completed in the forward berth is *Malte*, the first of two 8,222-ton cargo-passenger ships built for the French company Chargeur Reunis. *[Middle: George Scott Collection; bottom: Ian Rae Collection]*

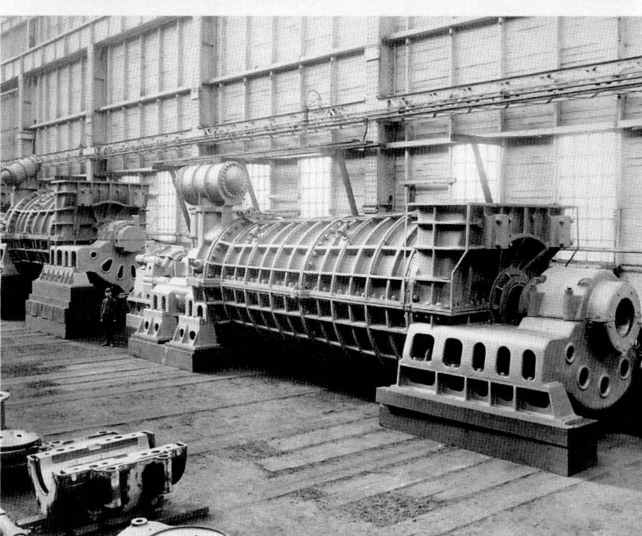

This series of images show the complexity and scale of *Mauretania*'s machinery. On launch day guests were taken on a tour of the engineering works and driven through the funnels, between the boilers (middle left) and along the line of turbines. The latter consisted of millions of blades, each produced to strict specifications on a manually operated machine. A fully bladed low-pressure turbine rotor is shown top right whilst a set of turbines can be seen middle right. The four elliptically shaped funnels were almost 70 feet high and were also laid out for view on 20th September 1906. *[Top left and middle right: Tyne and Wear Archives; top right, middle left and bottom: Zogolovitch Collection]*

Starboard engine starting platform. *[Zogolovitch Collection]*

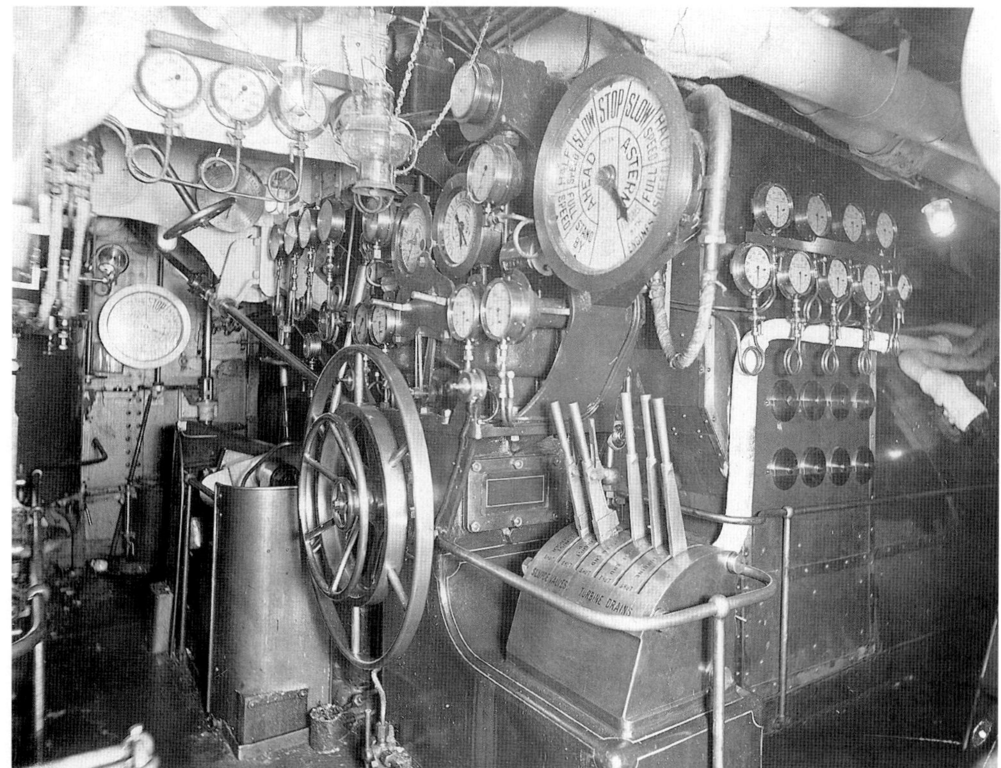

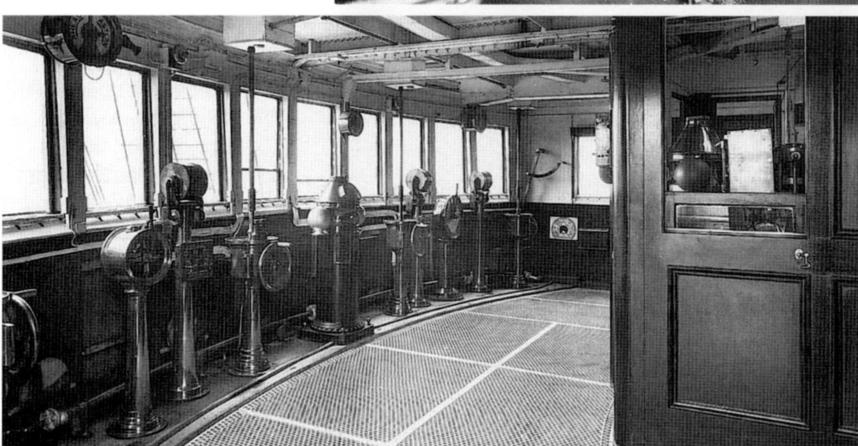

Left: View of the bridge from port, with the wheelhouse on the right. Note the camber of the deck. *[Zogolovitch Collection]*

Below: *Mauretania*'s first commander, Captain Pritchard, standing on the port bridge wing. He retired in 1909. *[Ambrose Greenway Collection]*

Mauretania and *Lusitania*'s original propellers had three rounded blades individually attached to a central boss. In 1908 further experimentation was done to find an improved design which would not only reduce vibration but would also increase the overall speed. A solid propeller with four pointed blades emerged as the most efficient solution and for a period in 1909 *Mauretania* ran with the new ones on the outer wings and the original type on the inner wings. Later in 1909 the four-bladed type was fitted on both ships. For the next 20 years *Mauretania* was unbeatable. *[Tyne & Wear Archives]*

Left and bottom left: *Mauretania* in 1909 with four-bladed propellers on the outer wings and the original three-bladed type on the inner wings. The photograph on the left shows the narrowness of her hull and the balanced rudder. The gentleman in uniform is *Mauretania*'s first Chief Engineer, John Currie. Note the slight damage to one of the blades of the inner starboard propeller, whilst another blade appears to have been a replacement. *[Tyne & Wear Archives]*

Below: With her four-bladed screws in dry dock during her 1926/27 refit. *[Peter Newall Collection]*

The record breaker 1907-1913

On 17th September 1907, just under a year after she was launched, *Mauretania* was towed down the Tyne to start her preliminary trials in the North Sea. Much to the dismay of local Tyne tug owners, two powerful L. Smit & Co. tugs were hired to take her down the Tyne into the North Sea. She was towed by *Poolzee* (304/1900) and escorted by *Oceaan* (394/1894). These Dutch tugs were also probably on emergency standby during *Mauretania*'s trials. With the reputation of both the shipyard and engine builders at stake the trials were conducted in great secrecy. She returned to the Tyne on 21st September for final fitting out and the painting of her hull in Cunard Line colours. Her sister *Lusitania* was originally painted white above the Shelter Deck, with a white band continuing along that deck to the bow. Contemporary artwork for *Mauretania* also showed a similar colour scheme. After her trials in June 1907, *Lusitania* had her black hull colour changed to include the forward plated section of the Shelter Deck and the forecastle. This paint scheme was also used for *Mauretania* and gave the two ships a more sleek and elongated appearance. Both liners were so well proportioned that it is often forgotten that they were the largest ships of their day and that the construction of liners over 30,000-tons did not happen for non-transatlantic routes until the 1950s and 1960s.

Fitting out was completed in October and on the 22nd *Mauretania* left the Tyne for her new home port Liverpool, with a party of distinguished guests aboard. She arrived there two days later on 24th October and entered the Canada Dock. The Mersey Docks and Harbour Board, fearful of loosing Cunard's prestigious new giants to Southampton, made a number of improvements to ensure a swift turnaround between voyages. The floating Prince's Landing Stage was given an upper deck whilst the surrounding area of river was dredged. At Rock Ferry, on the west side of the River Mersey, a large buoy at the Sloyne anchorage was provided so that the ships could be coaled without the need to enter the docks. At New York, a new Cunard Line passenger terminal was built at Pier 56 to accommodate the new liners.

After a week in dry dock *Mauretania* emerged on 30th October for coaling prior to her official trials. These began on the 3rd November and consisted of two return runs from Corsewall Light on the northern tip of the Galloway Peninsula, Scotland and the Longships Light at Land's End. These 48-hour steaming trials broke the existing speed record for a merchant ship and on the second run south she averaged a staggering 27.36 knots. On 6th November her coal consumption was tested on the Skelmorlie measured mile between Ailsa Craig and Holy Island, Scotland. On two of these runs she averaged a mean speed of 26.17 knots. Much to the relief of Swan, Hunter and Wigham Richardson and Wallsend Slipway and Engineering, the trials were deemed to be a great success and she was officially handed over to Cunard Line on 12th November 1907. *Lusitania*, meanwhile, had been delivered on 27th August and in October beat the German transatlantic record in both directions and reclaimed the Blue Riband for Britain after a gap of almost ten years.

Mauretania's maiden voyage to New York commenced on Saturday 16th November. Attempting to break the transatlantic record during the winter was always going to be a challenge and because of fog she completed the journey

Preliminary No 735 Trial Trip of — St Abbs Head Mile — Mauretania — Sept 19th 1907

High water Leith ·04pm / " " N Shields ·36pm

Draft forward leaving 28-3 return 27-2 Aft. 32-8 / 33-1 Mean. 30-5½ / 30-1½ / 30-3½ Disp. 33940 / 33500 / 33720 / for trim 170 / 33890 Co-ef. ·585 Mid Area. 2519ø

Condition Before dry docking vessel had been lying 1 year in the Tyne

Propeller dia. 17'-0" Mean Pitch. 15'-9" Blades. Three Surface. 92ø Wind. Sea Smooth Dead Calm N after 6th run went up to SNW

No. of Runs.	1	2	3	4	5	6	7	8	9	10
Time of day	12 noon	12·40pm	1-17pm	1-42pm	2-5pm	2·32pm	3pm	3·18pm	4·23	
Run N. or S.	S	N	S	N	S	N	S	N	S	
Tide	W	A	W	A	W	A	W	A		
Time on Mile	3-1	3-13½	2·37	2-53½	2·28	2-35	2·20	2·29	2-33⅖	
Speed	19·88	18·60	22·95	20·72	24·35	23·22	25·73	24·18	23·46	
(mean)	19·24		21·83		23·78		24·95			
I.H.P.	26832	28229	39015	39672	51204	54961	64225	63690		
Revolutions	131		150·3		166·3		177		162	
Mean Slip %	5·52		6·11		8·01		9·38			
Vacuum Port	27	27	27·2	27·5	27·0	28·0	27·8	27·8		
Vacuum Stbd	27½	27	28·0	28·0	29·0	28·0	28·0	28·0		
Boiler Steam in Engs P	186	187	180	185	174	184	182	182		
Boiler Steam in Engs S	185	187	180	185	174	185	182	183		
Steam Pipe in ER P	184	185	177	183	170	180	178	178		
Steam Pipe in ER S	183	185	177	183	169	180	177	177		
Steam Pipe at HP P	65	66	92	90	110	118	139	138		
Receiver S	58	65	84	80	110	118	129	129		
Compd. Gauge										

With a helm angle of 15° vessel went over to about 6°

HB

Log book recording her preliminary trials from St. Abb's Head in which she achieved almost 26 knots. *[Tyne & Wear Archives]*

in 5 days, 18 hours and 17 minutes at an average speed of only 22.21 knots. She remained in New York for just over a week and sailed to Liverpool on Saturday 30th November. On this voyage, despite some rough weather, she shaved twenty minutes off *Lusitania*'s eastbound record of 4 days, 22 hours and 53 minutes. The sibling rivalry between *Mauretania* and her older sister struck a cord with the British public and was the start of an illustrious career, in which *Mauretania* became one of the most famous and best-loved liners of the 20th century. However, there was also some negative comment about the way she behaved in rough weather. With stabilisers and pod propulsion, modern cruise ships are so steady that it is hard to imagine being aboard a ship which pitched and rolled as it ploughed through the waves with its knife-like bow. *Mauretania* was definitely a 'wet ship' with water frequently spraying over the bridge.

On her seventh crossing *Mauretania* left Liverpool on 2nd May 1908. About 250 miles outbound from Queenstown (later known as Cobh), Ireland she hit a submerged object, which sheered off a blade from her port outer wing propeller. In the mishap the large A-shaped bracket, which carried the propeller and its shaft, also fractured. Despite her three-legged state, she completed the voyage to New York at an average speed of 24.87 knots. Over the next five months, the engineers from Swan, Hunter and Wigham Richardson and Wallsend Slipway and Engineering experimented with various types of propeller design. More than 24 sets of three-bladed propellers and 17 sets of four-bladed propellers were tested on the electrically-driven model launch used for her original design. One of the main reasons for the tests was to further reduce vibration, which was already much better than other fast transatlantic liners. Most vibration on this type of ship was caused by propeller design rather than by the engines. Meanwhile, *Mauretania* continued to operate on three screws and at the end of October she entered the dry dock in Liverpool for repair work. Not only was she given a new A-frame bracket, but also new four-bladed propellers. The new screws were solid as opposed to the original ones which had individual blades attached to a central boss. These were fitted to the port and starboard outer wings whilst the original three-bladed inner propellers were retained. Some time later, these were also replaced with four-bladed solid propellers.

Mauretania's first sailing to New York with her new propellers was on 24th January 1909. At the end of the return voyage on February 8th she broke her own eastbound record: Sandy Hook (New York) to Daunt's Rock (Queenstown, Ireland) in 4 days, 20 hours and 27 minutes at an average speed of 25.16 knots. In June she shaved another three hours and six minutes off the record. Propellers of the same design were also fitted to *Lusitania* and she too improved her performance significantly. However, *Mauretania* always had the edge over her for speed. On September 9th 1909, despite fog and coal which was full of stones, she beat *Lusitania*'s westbound record by seven minutes and claimed the crown for the fastest-ever crossing: 4 days, 11 hours and 35 minutes. For the next twenty years she held the position as the world's fastest liner and Blue Riband champion of the North Atlantic.

Over the next three years from 1909 to 1911 *Mauretania* remained in continuous service without a major refit. She crossed the Atlantic 88 times, the majority of the voyages averaging over 25 knots. She also frequently beat her best times and for a brief spell in March 1910 attained a speed of 27.48 knots. It should be noted that she crossed the Atlantic on different courses, depending on the time of year. Choosing the best route across the North Atlantic is always challenging because of the weather. In winter months eastward-sweeping stormy areas of low pressure are avoided by taking the longer southerly route. Ideally, the shortest route is a great circle path. However, in spring and early summer this course is threatened by Greenland's icebergs swept south by the Labrador Current into the warm flow of the Gulf Stream. After the *Titanic* disaster in April 1912, the number of lifeboats on *Mauretania* increased from eight sets either side to nine. There were also numerous deck lifeboats. These were flat-packed lifeboats with collapsible sides stowed to save space on deck. In her post-war guise the number of lifeboats on *Mauretania* was increased to 12 sets either side.

In 1906 the small town of Fishguard on the south west coast of Wales became the Great Western Railway's main departure point for the short sea crossing to Ireland. The GWR ran regular rail services between Paddington and the newly developed harbour. In 1909 Cunard Line decided that its express liners would stop at Fishguard as well as Queenstown in southern Ireland for eastbound crossings. This meant that passengers and the mails could reach London at least half a day earlier than travelling via Liverpool. *Mauretania* made Cunard Line's first call on 30th August 1909 and landed the London mail and 240 passengers with their baggage. In 1912 Cunard Line announced a change in *Mauretania* and *Lusitania*'s eastbound schedule. Liners would leave New York on Wednesday morning without calling at Queenstown so that passengers could reach London on Monday afternoon and Paris the same evening. In 1914 Queenstown was dropped in both directions.

In June 1911 *Mauretania* lost her place as the world's largest ship when *Olympic* entered service as the first of three 45,000-ton liners built for White Star Line . Cunard Line responded with the 45,647-ton *Aquitania*, which was completed in May 1914. This new liner allowed Cunard Line to briefly operate a three ship express service to New York. Although *Aquitania*, *Olympic* and *Titanic* were undoubtedly impressive ships, their large public rooms and ostentatious decoration had none of the style or human scale of *Mauretania*'s interiors.

The amount of coal required for a single trip between Liverpool and New York was phenomenal. It was the equivalent of 20 trains of 30 trucks, each truck containing 10 tons. *[Zogolovitch Collection]*

On the 17th September 1907 *Mauretania* left the Tyne for preliminary trials in the North Sea. She was towed by the powerful Dutch ocean-going tug *Poolzee* and escorted by her two-funnelled fleet mate *Oceaan*. *[Top: George Scott Collection; bottom: Ambrose Greenway Collection]*

Above: The start of her trial run was St. Abb's Head, Berwickshire and this rare photo shows her at full speed passing St. Abb's Head Lighthouse. *[George Scott Collection]*

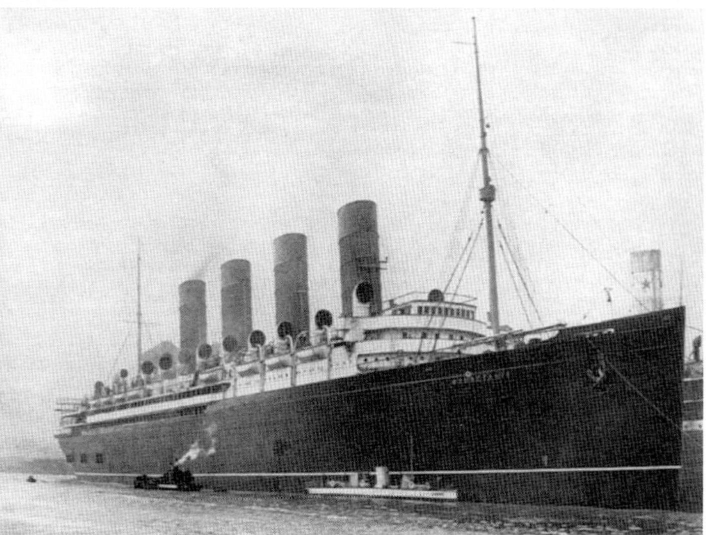

Turbinia alongside the completed *Mauretania.*

CUNARD LINE

R.M.S. "MAURETANIA," OCTOBER 23rd, 1907

. . . . BREAKFAST. . . . .

Melon Apples Oranges French Plums

Rolled Oats Oatmeal Porridge

Fried Fillets of Plaice Findon Haddock Fresh Herrings

Eggs :—Boiled, Fried Poached, and Scrambled

Hamburg Steak Kidney and Bacon

Cumberland Ham Wiltshire Bacon

Potatoes—Fried and Saute

To order from Grill :--

Sirloin Steak—Maitre d'Hotel Mutton Chops

Fresh Rolls Vienna Bread Soda Scones

Banana Fritters

Marmalade Preserves

Tea Coffee Cocoa

This remarkable menu shows the first breakfast served aboard *Mauretania* the morning after she left Newcastle. Interestingly, the image of the ship shows her with the initial hull colour scheme which was intended for the two new liners. *[Paul Louden-Brown Collection]*

On the return from her builder's trials, *Mauretania*'s grey hull was painted in Cunard Line's black hull livery. She left the Tyne on her delivery voyage to Liverpool on the afternoon of 22nd October. This evocative image shows her towed by the Tyne tugs *Washington* (124/1870) and *President* (130/1876). *[Bottom: George Scott Collection; middle: World Ship Society Collection]*

Belching black smoke, *Mauretania* set the record for the world's fastest merchant ship during her official trials in November 1907. *[Top: Ian Rae Collection; bottom: Zogolovitch Collection]*

Port side of *Mauretania* on her official trials with the B Deck promenade protected by awnings. *[Tyne & Wear Archives]*

Although they were sisters, there were distinct differences between *Mauretania* (top) and *Lusitania* as shown in these trials photos. The most obvious on *Mauretania* were the more rounded and less stepped bridge front, overhang on the Boat and Promenade Decks, large ventilator cowls and longer forecastle spirket plate. *Lusitania* was originally painted white above the Shelter Deck but after her trials this was changed, with the black extended one deck higher. This gave the ship a more powerful and impressive appearance. *[Bob Bradshaw Collection]*

Early years in Liverpool

Left: Manoeuvring *Mauretania* in the enclosed Liverpool Docks always required great skill from the tug and dock masters. Here she is entering the Sandon Dock. *[Bob Bradshaw Collection]*

Right: In the Sandon Half-Tide Dock entrance lock, the gentleman with the megaphone is probably the Lock Master. In the distance is his office, which still exists today. *[Ken Saunders Collection]*

Lusitania is being towed past *Mauretania* in the Sandon Half Tide Dock. Alongside, pushing up, is Cunard's passenger tender *Skirmisher. [Bob Bradshaw Collection]*

Left: Sunset and *Mauretania*. *[Bob Bradshaw Collection]*

Middle: Because she had to be coaled on both sides, coaling was done in the River Mersey at the Sloyne buoy. This was a slow and messy process and promenade areas had to be covered with awnings. *[Ian Farquhar Collection]*

Right: Passengers and crew were also transported by tender when the ship was unable to cross the bar or as here, in mid-river off Rock Ferry. Note the open Second Class promenade on B Deck. This was later given bulwarks in place of open rails. *[Bob Bradshaw Collection]*

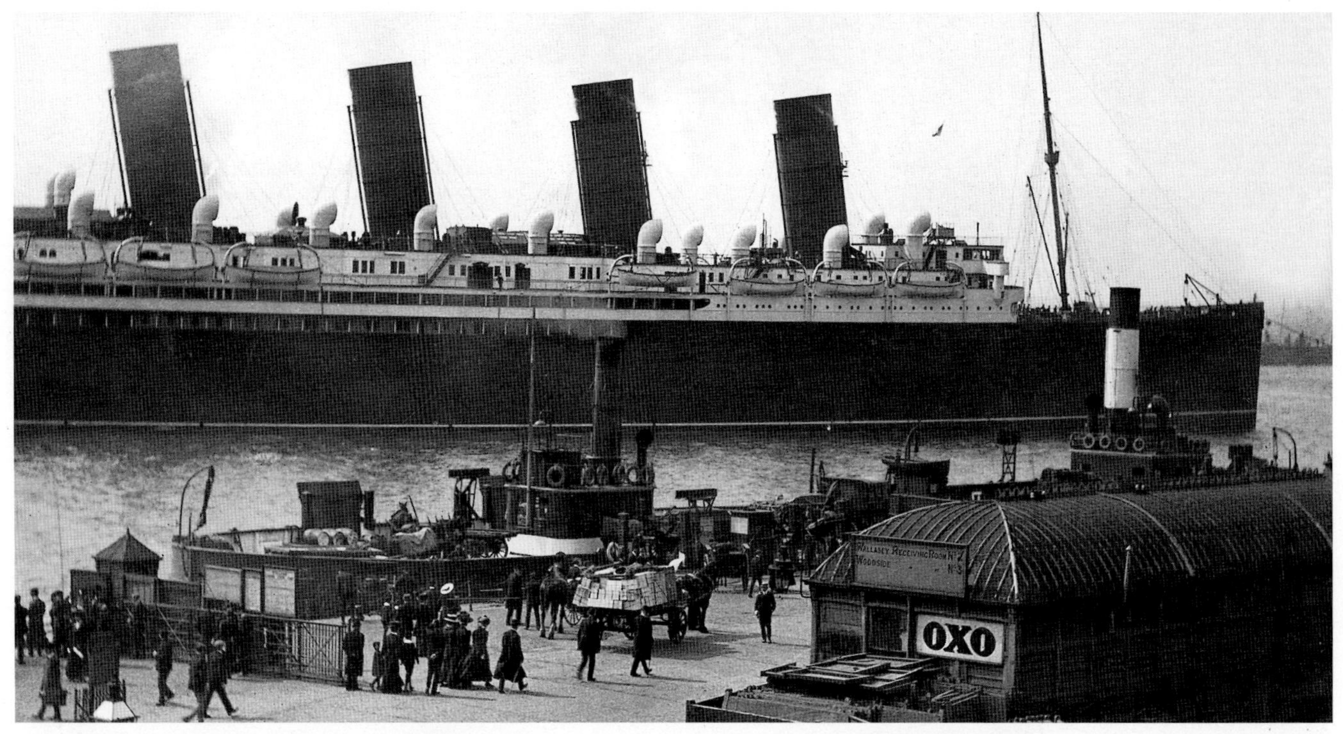

In the River Mersey the tides can fluctuate by as much as 34 feet. The 2,534-foot floating Princes' Landing Stage allowed passengers to embark and disembark with the rise and fall of the tide. To accommodate Cunard's new giants, an upper level with connecting gangways was added in 1906. Alongside the landing stage was the Riverside Station where the London and North Western Railway ran special express trains to and from London's Euston Station. This integrated service, with guaranteed seating, offered a journey time between Liverpool and London of less than four hours. Passengers were also able to pass from train to ship without being exposed to the weather. Above: *Mauretania* is moving alongside the landing stage, with the other photos showing her berthed. Note the covered gangway and Riverside Station. *[Top and bottom: Bob Bradshaw Collection; middle: Peter Newall Collection]*

Above and left: On 11th July 1913 King George V and Queen Mary, accompanied by Prince Edward, aboard the Mersey Docks and Harbour Board's tender *Galatea* opened the new Gladstone Dock. Among the 35 ships on display in the River Mersey was *Mauretania*, which was inspected by the royal party. *[Top: Peter Newall Collection; right: Bob Bradshaw Collection]*

"FLAP" KITTEN
RESCUED FROM
S.S. "WEST POINT"
DESTROYED BY
FIRE AUG. 27TH
1910.
PICKED UP
TOGETHER WITH
16 OF THE CREW
BY R.M.S.
"MAURETANIA" SEPT. 2ND 1910.

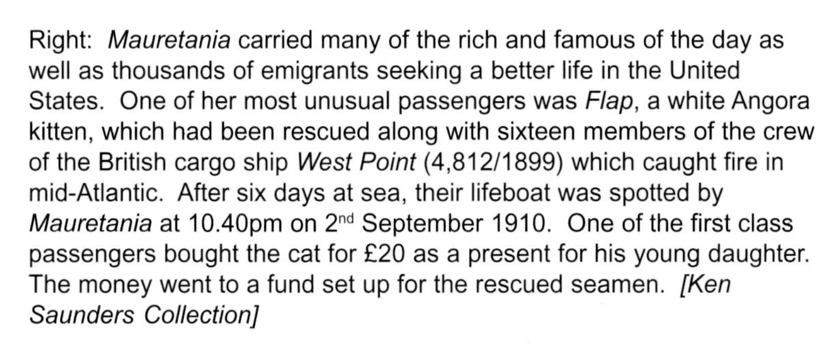

Right: *Mauretania* carried many of the rich and famous of the day as well as thousands of emigrants seeking a better life in the United States. One of her most unusual passengers was *Flap*, a white Angora kitten, which had been rescued along with sixteen members of the crew of the British cargo ship *West Point* (4,812/1899) which caught fire in mid-Atlantic. After six days at sea, their lifeboat was spotted by *Mauretania* at 10.40pm on 2nd September 1910. One of the first class passengers bought the cat for £20 as a present for his young daughter. The money went to a fund set up for the rescued seamen. *[Ken Saunders Collection]*

Above: *Mauretania* in dock at Seaforth. *[Bob Bradshaw Collection]*

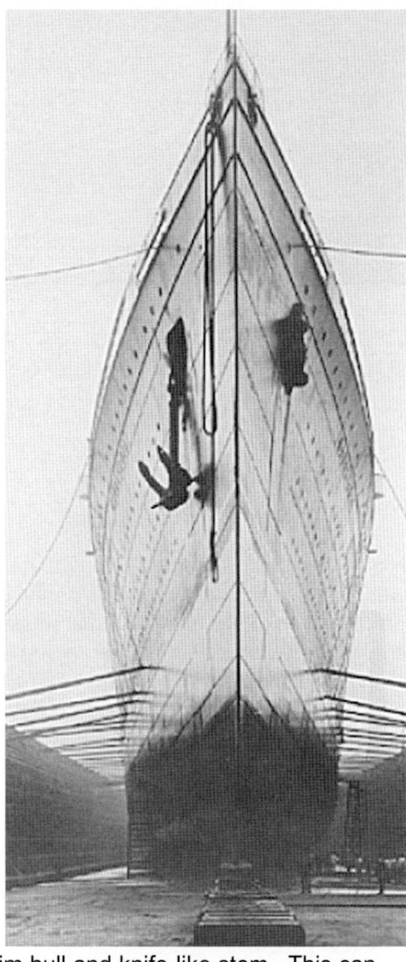

Above: Another reason for *Mauretania*'s record-breaking speed was the design of her slim hull and knife-like stem. This can be clearly seen in these two photos of her in dry dock. On the left, she is being painted in the Canada Graving Dock. *[Left: Michael Pocock Collection; Right: A. Andrews Collection]*

Mauretania arrives at Fishguard on 30th August 1909. This was Cunard Line's first call at the port. *[Paul Louden-Brown Collection]*

Leaving Liverpool for New York on 16th May 1914 shortly before the outbreak of the First World War. *[Fred Hawkes Collection]*

This early view shows *Mauretania* and the impressive New York skyline. Her name appears to have been retouched on the photograph. *[Tyne & Wear Archives]*

The war years 1914 to 1918

On the 28th of June 1914, the heir to the Austro-Hungarian throne, Archduke Franz Ferdinand, was assassinated at Sarajevo. Over the next five weeks, the subsequent chain of events led to the outbreak of the First World War. Unrest loomed over Europe, as *Mauretania* sailed from Liverpool on 1st August, on what was to be her last peacetime voyage for four years. On 4th August Britain declared war on Germany and the following day *Mauretania* was told the news in an Admiralty wireless telegraph sent from the Marconi Station at Poldhu, Cornwall. On 6th August she received instructions from the armoured cruiser *HMS Essex* to head for Halifax, Nova Scotia.

In early August the Admiralty informed Cunard Line that the liners *Carmania*, *Caronia*, *Mauretania*, *Lusitania* and the recently completed *Aquitania* were required for conversion into armed merchant cruisers. Soon after it was announced that neither *Mauretania* nor *Lusitania* would be needed. They continued to ply the Liverpool-New York route. Although the sisters *Carmania* and *Caronia* became successful armed merchant cruisers, *Aquitania* was deemed too big for this role and later in the war she was used as a troop transport and hospital ship. Size was also the most likely factor for not requisitioning *Mauretania* and *Lusitania* in 1914.

Between 29th August and 21st October 1914 *Mauretania* made three transatlantic crossings in tandem with *Lusitania*. Although initial westbound passenger loads averaged around 1,500, these soon fell as the conflict worsened on mainland Europe. By October the numbers carried were less than 1,000 and Cunard decided to withdraw *Mauretania*, leaving *Lusitania* to soldier on as Cunard's sole express liner. This was a fateful decision: on 7th May, 1915 she was sunk off the Old Head of Kinsale, Ireland by the German submarine *U 20*. The loss of 1,198 lives caused an outrage on both sides of the Atlantic and ensured that Germany could no longer look to the United States for support. It also showed the vulnerability of large liners to submarines. With all their vital equipment below the waterline, *Lusitania* and her sister had of course been designed to resist attack from surface gunfire and not from torpedoes.

The hospital ship *Mauretania*. [J. & M. Clarkson collection]

At the start of 1915, with the war on the Western Front at a stalemate, Britain turned its attention to Turkey, Germany's ally in the Eastern Mediterranean. If the Gallipoli Peninsula on the western shore of the Dardanelles could be taken, Constantinople would fall and Turkey would be knocked out of the war. A new Eastern Front could then be opened up with the combined force of Allied and Russian troops. However, the British leaders underestimated the resolve and skill of the Turkish military commanders. From start to finish, the campaign was a disaster and cost the lives of over half a million men on both sides of the conflict. After the failure of a naval attack in February, British, Australian and New Zealand troops landed on the Aegean side of the Gallipoli Peninsula on 25th April 1915.

Reinforcements were soon required and *Mauretania*, which had been laid up at Liverpool since October 1914, was requisitioned as a troop transport by the Admiralty Transport Service on 11th May 1915. Her fittings and furniture were removed and placed in storage. Bunks and hammocks were then installed in the public rooms for up to 4,000 troops. Her funnels and portholes were painted black whilst her upperworks received a coat of grey paint.

In her new role, she left Liverpool on 21st May for the Allied base at Mudros Bay on the north Aegean Greek island of Lemnos. Aboard were over 3,000 soldiers. On her second voyage to Lemnos a six-inch gun had been installed on her stern. She sailed from Liverpool on the 9th July carrying 3,644 troops and 60 nurses and arrived at Mudros Bay a week later. She departed for England on 23rd July and, two hours into her voyage, a lookout in the crow's nest spotted a submarine's periscope. The enemy submarine, which had been lying in wait, fired two torpedoes. It was only through swift evasive action from the bridge that they both missed, one by thirty feet and the other by a mere five feet. However, a few hours after this amazing escape, just before 3am in blacked out conditions, she was struck on the starboard side by the British tramp steamer *Cardiff Hall* (3,994/1912). Although the cargo ship had her bow stoved in, *Mauretania* was fortunate enough to only suffer minor damage to her hull plates. Two members of *Cardiff Hall*'s crew with slight injuries were transferred to *Mauretania* and put ashore at Malta the next day.

Because of the submarine attack near Lemnos and increased submarine activity in the Mediterranean, *Mauretania* was dazzle-painted for her final Gallipoli trooping voyage on 25th August. Large diamond-shaped patterns in grey and white were painted on her hull, ventilators and funnels. The purpose of this type of naval camouflage was to confuse the enemy as to the identity of the ship and the direction it was travelling. How effective it was in bright sunlight on a calm sea was a moot point. In addition, *Mauretania*, with her great speed, usually sailed on a zigzag course when in dangerous waters. She returned to Liverpool on 5th October, having transported 10,391 troops during her three voyages to the Eastern Mediterranean.

Casualties at Gallipoli were very high and dysentery was rife. To bring the large number of wounded and sick soldiers home, three of Britain's premier liners were converted into hospital ships in the latter part of 1915. These were *Britannic*, the third of White Star Line's *Olympic*-class of giant liners, *Aquitania* and *Mauretania*. *Mauretania*'s conversion into a hospital ship took place in Liverpool. Public rooms were changed into wards and fitted with beds and cots, whilst other areas became operating theatres and pharmacies. The open first and second class promenade spaces were also glassed in to form wards. Once the work was complete she had a capacity for 2,154 patients and 350 medical staff. Externally she was painted white with red boot-topping. Her funnels were buff whilst a deep green band with large red crosses ran either side of her hull. The cost of the conversion work was £68,000.

HMHS Mauretania departed from Liverpool on 22nd October for Lemnos and over the next three months embarked 6,307 patients at Mudros Bay, some of whom succumbed during the voyage. Southampton became her home base and she sailed from there on 23rd November and 7th January 1916. She arrived back at Southampton on 25th January and remained there for almost a month awaiting a decision about her future. By then the Gallipoli campaign was almost over and Allied troops were being withdrawn from the war zone. As she was no longer needed as a hospital ship, she returned to the Mersey on 25th February. Her hospital fittings were dismantled and she was paid off from Government Service on 1st March. Cunard Line was given £60,000 to cover refurbishment costs.

At the end of September 1916, *Mauretania* was again requisitioned as a troopship, this time to carry Canadian troops for the Western Front. Transformed into a trooper and given a 12-pounder gun forward of the foremast and a six-inch gun aft, *HMT Mauretania* sailed from Liverpool to Halifax on 12th October. Another round voyage to Halifax followed a month later on 12th November. In all, 6,212 troops were brought over between October and November. After a period of lay up in the Gladstone Dock, Liverpool, she was moved to the Clyde and arrived at Greenock on 20th February 1917. For the remainder of 1917 she was laid up in Gare Loch, on the north side of the Clyde.

The turning point in the First World War came on 6th April 1917 when the United States entered the war against Germany. Thousands of troops poured into Europe throughout 1917 and on 10th January 1918 *Mauretania* returned to Liverpool for reactivation as a troopship. Her first voyage from Liverpool to New York was on 10th March. Monthly sailings followed on 9th April, 14th May, 11th June, 17th July and 17th August. The final voyage before Armistice Day on 11th of November took place in October. On that trip she sailed from New York with over 4,000 troops in the first week of November and was at sea when war's end was declared. These troops disembarked and were quartered in Liverpool before re-embarking on *Mauretania* 25th November, arriving back in New York on 1st December. She was the first ship to sail westbound with American soldiers after the signing of the Armistice. Between March and November 1918, *Mauretania* carried almost 34,000 United States troops to Europe. During this final phase of her wartime career, *Mauretania* was at last fitted with the guns she was designed to carry. These included four six-inch guns on her fore deck and two on her stern.

As an armed troopship, she also appears to have been painted in at least three dazzle-paint schemes. One was the 1915 harlequin-type design with large diamonds but with the possible addition of red, blue and yellow colours whilst the other had diamond shapes forward and stripes aft. The third was a more traditional, stripy dazzle pattern. She was also reported to have been named *HMS Tuberose*. As there was already a *HMS Tuberose* in Royal Navy service, this was probably a joke on *Mauretania*'s rather sombre commander, Captain Rostron, who mentioned this fact in his autobiography. With a displacement tonnage of only 1,290 the 1917-built sloop *HMS Tuberose* was one of the smallest in the Royal Navy. However, she too came from Swan, Hunter and Wigham Richardson, which is possibly the reason the Admiralty wits chose this name.

Painting by Burnett Poole of *Mauretania* in her original dazzle colour scheme, escorted by destroyers. *[Ambrose Greenway Collection]*

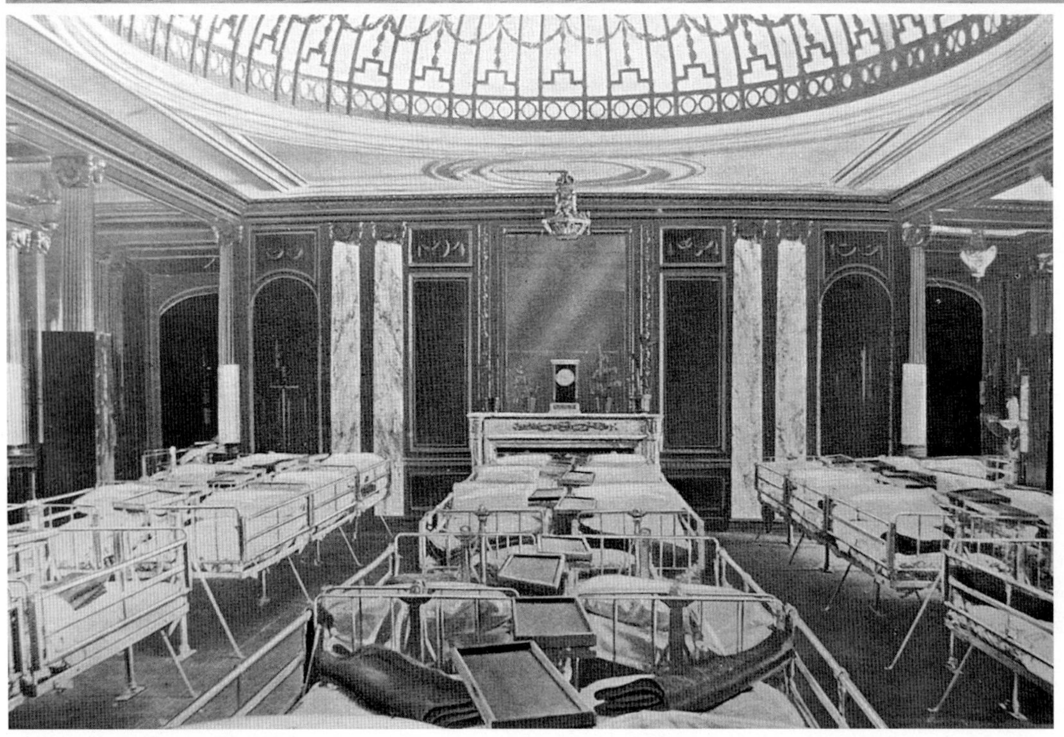

Top: Mauretania's first call at Mudros as a troopship was in May 1915. Her funnels were painted black whilst her upperworks were grey. *[Imperial War Museum Q13816]* Middle and bottom: Between October 1915 and January 1916 she operated as the hospital ship *HMHS Mauretania*. The open first and second class promenade spaces were glassed in to form wards. Beds were also fitted in the First Class Lounge. *[Top: Imperial War Museum Q13608; bottom: Peter Newall Collection]*

Great Cunard Liner "Mauretania," Holder of the "Blue Rib

CLUDING HER OWN BANK AND NEWSPAPER PRINTING OFFICES: THE INTERIOR (STARBOA

refit, during which she was again completely overhauled, while many improvements and extensions were made in the structure and decoration
Transatlantic service. The "Mauretania" is one of the most popular ships engaged in that service. She is supreme as an "ocean greyhound," ar
passengers arrive regularly in London within five-and-a-half days of leaving New York. When the war broke out the "Mauretania" rushe
ioned, and oil replaced coal as fuel. Her 2300 passengers are carried in the greatest comfort, no matter whether they are travelling firs

CARRYING ALL THE AMENITIES OF A TOWN ON THE HIGH SEAS, IN

The great Cunard liner "Mauretania," holder of the Atlantic speed record, has lately resumed another season's work after a very thorough the passenger quarters. After a first trip from Southampton to New York, she started on a Mediterranean cruise before returning to the recently broke all Atlantic records—which were, incidentally, her own—by crossing the Atlantic at an average speed of 26·25 knots. Her home across the Atlantic, and thereafter played many useful parts. On the conclusion of hostilities she was overhauled and recondit

In 1915 and 1918 she appears to have been painted in at least four dazzle-paint schemes. Top: For her final voyage to Mudros as a troopship in 1915 she was given a harlequin-type design with large diamonds. Middle left: As an armed merchant cruiser in 1918. She had the same pattern but with the possible addition of red, blue and yellow colours. Bottom: She also had diamond shapes forward and stripes aft and a more traditional, stripy dazzle scheme: middle right. *[Top: Imperial War Museum Q21493; middle left: Tyne and Wear Archives; bottom: Peter Newall Collection]*

Mauretania made two voyages as a troopship to Halifax in October and November 1916. She was given a 12-pounder gun forward of the foremast, the base of which can be seen in this photo of her embarking troops at Pier 2, Halifax on either 23rd or 24th November 1916. *[Ambrose Greenway Collection]*

At war's end she repatriated thousands of Canadian troops. Here she is leaving Southampton, repainted in peacetime colours. *[Peter Newall Collection]*

On the 1st December 1918 *Mauretania* arrived in New York with the first of almost 34,000 United States homeward bound troops who she would carry over the next year. These men had gone only as far as Liverpool as they were travelling aboard *Mauretania* when the Armistice was declared. *[Top: Michael Pocock Collection; middle and bottom: Peter Newall Collection]*

Peace and the end of coal burning 1919 to 1922

On Christmas Eve 1918 *Mauretania* made her first peacetime sailing from Southampton to New York with 268 first class and 270 second class passengers, mainly on Government service. En route, she called at Brest to embark 3,167 returning United States troops. Southampton became the homeport for Cunard Line's express liners in February 1919 when Cunard's Chairman Sir Alfred Booth announced that it would take over the Southampton-Cherbourg-New York route formally operated by the main German lines. Despite this change, *Mauretania* and the rest of the fleet remained registered at Liverpool.

Mauretania spent much of 1919 assisting in the repatriation of thousands of United States and Canadian troops. For the 27th February and 31st March sailings to New York she called at Brest, each time picking up around 3,500 United States troops. On 4th May she made the first of a series of voyages to New York via Halifax where she disembarked Canadian service personnel. Despite being paid off from Government Service at Liverpool on 23rd May, her next two voyages to New York, including her last sailing from Liverpool on 1st June, went via Halifax with troops. On her return to England in July she was given a comprehensive post-war refit and commenced her first commercial sailing on 20th September 1919 with 366 first class, 179 second class and 181 third class passengers. The following departure on 18th October saw the final call at Halifax with troops and on the 18th November she at last inaugurated the Southampton-Cherbourg-New York service.

For much of 1920 *Mauretania* bore the brunt of Cunard Line's express operation. Not only was demand high for first and second class berths in the post-war passenger resurgence but both *Aquitania* and Cunard's latest acquisition, *Berengaria*, the former German liner *Imperator*, were out of service for lengthy periods, undergoing major refits. *Aquitania* was converted from coal to oil firing at a time when good quality coal was at a premium. This meant that *Mauretania*, using inferior foreign coal, was unable to attain her record-breaking pre-war speeds. Average speeds had fallen from just over 23 knots to around 20 knots. Things were made worse by the fact that the quality of stokers had also declined since the war and the men had become more belligerent. This was, of course, a time of great social change in Britain. The Edwardian era into which *Mauretania* was born had become a distant memory as workers sought improved working conditions and greater stability of employment.

After a lengthy refit she sailed for New York on 26th March 1921. On that occasion the average speed for the crossing was less than 20 knots. For a vessel, which still held the transatlantic record after 14 years, this was not an impressive performance. Something had to be done and, on 25th July 1921, an event occurred which forced Cunard Line to make a decision about *Mauretania*'s long term future. During a routine turnaround at Southampton and with a skeleton crew aboard, a fire broke out in one of the first class cabins on D Deck. It had been caused by a careless workman using petrol to clean a carpet. The blaze soon spread and most of the cabins beneath the First Class Dining Saloon were destroyed. The parquet floor of the Dining Saloon was also badly damaged, as was some of the woodwork and carpets. The damage was so severe that it was decided to withdraw *Mauretania* from service and send her back to Newcastle in September for a major refurbishment, which would also include, at long last, her conversion from coal to oil firing. The work by Swan, Hunter and Wigham Richardson cost a quarter of a million pounds and included a complete refurbishment of her passenger accommodation. The area on D Deck housing 192 stokers was revamped for use by other crew members. This freed up space for extra cabins in First Class, many of which now had en-suite facilities. Improvements were also made in Second Class and Third Class. The capacity changes were: First Class up from 563 to 589 whilst Second Class and Third Class numbers were reduced from 475 to 392 and from 1,138 to 767 respectively. The last mentioned was reduced mainly because of new legislation restricting immigration into the United States. Between 1921 and 1922 the number of emigrants carried by Cunard Line fell by a third.

The work in *Mauretania*'s engine room was undertaken by the Wallsend Slipway and Engineering Co. Ltd. Although she was originally designed to be converted at some stage in her career from coal to oil, it was an immense job and took almost five months to complete. Fifteen oil tanks, with a total capacity of 5,350 tons, and two filling stations were fitted each side. After the refit she left the Tyne on 11th March 1922, her gross tonnage reduced to 30,696 . The impact of the new changes was dramatic. She departed from Southampton for New York on 25th March and the average speed for the crossing was just under 24 knots. This compared with 18.6 knots for her last westbound trip as a coal burner. Bunkering was also now a relatively simple job compared with the nightmare of coaling and the accompanying clouds of dust, which invaded every open space on the ship. At the end of April she made the fastest crossing from New York to France: 5 days, 1 hour and 23 minutes at an average speed of 25.14 knots.

Cruising and the loss of the Blue Riband 1923 to 1929

Another turning point in *Mauretania*'s career came on 7th February 1923 when she left New York with 531 wealthy American passengers on her first-ever cruise. She had been chartered by the American Express Company of New York for a five-week cruise around the Mediterranean. With prices starting at $950, she operated as a first class-only ship and made calls at Madeira, Gibraltar, Algiers, Monte Carlo, Naples, Athens, Constantinople, Haifa and Alexandria. American Express entered the travel business in 1915 when it established The American Express Travel Department. In 1919 its first escorted tourists to Europe crossed the Atlantic aboard *Mauretania* and in 1922 it organised the first world cruise when it chartered Cunard Line's brand-new *Laconia*. The success of *Mauretania*'s Mediterranean cruise led to it becoming an annual event between 1925 and 1930.

A major reason for the 1921/1922 refit was the change from coal to oil firing. In November 1923 she was again withdrawn from service, this time for a complete overhaul of her 16-year-old turbines. John I. Thornycroft and Co. Ltd., the official repairers for Cunard Line at Southampton, was given the task of dismantling and renewing tens of thousands of turbine blades. The refit also included sliding windows fitted halfway along the first class promenade on B Deck and a major refurbishment of her passenger accommodation.

About half the turbine work had been completed in February 1924 when the shipyard engineers went on strike. *Mauretania*'s first post-refit voyage on 29th March was cancelled and, because the peak transatlantic season was about to start, it was decided to complete the work at Cherbourg. With her engines still in pieces, *Mauretania* was powerless and five Dutch tugs had to be hired to tow her across the English Channel. She left Southampton around 10.30am on Friday 11th April under charge of *Roode Zee* (573/1908), *Zwarte Zee* (604/1906), *Humber* (519/1907), *Schelde* (359/1926) and the tug which towed her down the Tyne for her trials in 1907, *Poolzee* (304/1900). These tugs belonged to L. Smit & Co.'s Internationale Sleepdienst of Rotterdam. The crossing should have taken just over 12 hours but, because of a westerly gale, she only reached Cherbourg at 7pm the following Sunday. She returned to Southampton in May and at the end of the month sailed for New York. During that voyage she lost a propeller when one of the outer shafts snapped. Despite having only three screws, she completed the homebound voyage and the following eastbound crossing at an average of over 24 knots. A new propeller was fitted in July and for the next departure to New York on 9th August she broke her own transatlantic record in both directions: Cherbourg-Ambrose Channel Light Vessel (New York), 4 days, 20 hours and 2 minutes at an average speed of 25.6 knots; Ambrose Channel Light Vessel-Cherbourg, 4 days and 19 hours at an average speed of 26.16 knots. On 7th April 1925 she made her first eastbound call at Plymouth in Devon before proceeding to Cherbourg. This allowed passengers bound for London to catch a Great Western train to the capital, arriving before *Mauretania* berthed at Southampton. On that occasion she arrived at Plymouth at 5.15am, sailed at 7am, then called at Cherbourg in the afternoon and reached Southampton at 6.30pm: three ports in one day.

Despite her record-breaking performance, *Mauretania* was about to face her greatest challenge with the impending arrival of new transatlantic liners under construction in Italy, France and Germany. As she approached her 20th birthday, she was sent on what was to be her final visit to Liverpool for another comprehensive refit. She arrived on 6th December 1926 and in the Canada Graving Dock underwent a two-month reconditioning of her passenger accommodation and engine machinery. Many of her first class staterooms were remodelled and provided with hot and cold running water. Double inner cabins were upgraded into singles whilst the main public rooms were given new carpets and curtains. The Verandah Café was also remodelled on the lines of the Orangery at Hampton Court. A new fuel bunker was added, raising her fuel capacity to 7,000 tons. A new propeller shaft and two new 18-ton propellers were also fitted.

On her return to Southampton in February 1927, the directors of Cunard Line optimistically hoped that she 'has a further 20 years of active service before her'. However, in June she was completely eclipsed by the arrival of French Line's 43,153-ton *Ile de France*. As *Mauretania* had done in her day, this liner represented the essence of the period, with ultra modern interiors, the likes of which had never been seen before on the Atlantic run. Despite this, *Ile de France* was no match for the old veteran's superior speed. In 1928, *Mauretania*'s final year as the transatlantic record holder, she again beat her best crossing times. Her Blue Riband crown was finally taken on 22nd July 1929 when Norddeutscher Lloyd's 51,656-ton *Bremen* arrived in New York on her maiden voyage. Her crossing from Cherbourg to the Ambrose Channel Light Vessel took 4 days, 17 hours and 42 minutes at an average speed of 27.83 knots. She beat *Mauretania*'s best time of September 1928 by a mere 56 minutes. Coincidentally, *Mauretania* was in port to witness her arrival. *Bremen* reinforced her superiority on the return voyage by claiming the eastbound record: Ambrose Channel Light Vessel-Eddystone Light in 4 days, 14 hours and 30 minutes at an average speed of 27.91 knots.

Between November 1928 and January 1929 *Mauretania* underwent a six-week refit to her engines, which included new condensers and pumps, and in August she made one last bid to regain her title. Although she was still slower in both directions than the German liner, her performance was remarkable for a 22-years old ship. Her times were: Cherbourg to the Ambrose Channel Light Vessel, 4 days, 21 hours and 44 minutes at an average speed of 26.85 knots; Ambrose Channel Light Vessel to Eddystone Light, 4 days, 17 hours and 50 minutes at an average speed of 27.22 knots.

Whilst leaving New York on 27th November 1929 *Mauretania* was in collision with a float carrying railway cars. Although no one was injured, she suffered some bow damage, which was soon repaired. This was one of the rare events which upset *Mauretania*'s schedule. Throughout her long career, she was a remarkably reliable ship. The only accident which involved fatalities occurred on 26th January 1914 when a gas cylinder exploded in her engine room during a refit, killing three workmen.

The final years 1930 to 1934

In October 1929 the gaiety and optimism of the 1920s was brought to a swift end with the Wall Street Crash and the onset of the Great Depression. The impact was especially bad on the Atlantic liner routes with ships travelling half full and many vessels laid up. In 1930 Cunard Line came under great economic pressure, especially after it placed an order in December with John Brown on the Clyde for a new giant liner to replace its ageing pre-war-built ships. Trading conditions were so bad that *Mauretania*'s annual Mediterranean cruise in February 1931 and one to Havana were cancelled. On April 24th she sailed on the first of a series of weekend cruises from New York. These were fitted in between transatlantic turnarounds. Instead of sitting in New York not earning any money, she sailed from New York at 5pm on Friday and returned at 3pm the following Tuesday. Prices ranged from $50 per person for a two-berth cabin to $300 per person in one of the B Deck Parlour Suites. For the duration of the cruise she operated as a one-class ship with those in the second class accommodation eating in the Second Class Dining Saloon but able to use all the first class facilities. A canvas pool was rigged and passengers were also able to enjoy 'sun-bathing... a fad which has swept the world in the last few years.' Between April and September seven of these weekend cruises operated, three to Nassau and four to Halifax. Longer cruises to the West Indies followed later that year, all out of New York. In 1932 she made eight cruises and ten transatlantic round trips and towards the end of the year it was decided that she would become a full-time cruise ship.

In May 1933 *Mauretania* underwent a one-month refit at Southampton for her new life as a cruise ship and emerged with a white hull. This was done for aesthetic as well as functional reasons. It reduced the ambient hull temperature by a few degrees, which in a ship not designed for tropical waters would have provided some relief from the heat. The foremast and derricks were also white whilst the top of the mainmast remained black for the simple reason that it was behind the funnels and would become smoke blackened.

The boot-topping was painted green as were the deckheads. Later the boot-topping was changed to red and her masts buff.

She also had facilities for 'talking pictures' and an 18 by 15-foot wooden swimming pool on A Deck, just forward of the Second Class Lounge. Her first voyage in her new colour scheme took place on Saturday 3rd June when she sailed from Southampton on the first of two short back-to-back cruises to Casablanca and Madeira. These were organised by Cunard as a cruise club, with a limited number of members. At the end of June she sailed for New York where she spent most of 1933 and 1934 cruising to the West Indies.

Meanwhile in December 1931 Cunard Line suspended construction of its unfinished 81,237-ton liner at Clydebank. Now, for the second time in thirty years, the future of Cunard Line became the focus of national attention. British prestige was at stake with Germany, France and Italy continuing to build ships, which threatened British supremacy on the North Atlantic. The British Government stepped in and offered Cunard a £9.5 million loan to complete the new *Queen Mary* and to build an even-larger running mate, the 83,673-ton *Queen Elizabeth*. A condition of this agreement was the merger in 1934 of Cunard Line and White Star Line to form a new company, Cunard White Star Ltd., commonly known as Cunard White Star Line. This meant a clearing out of older ships and near the top of the list was *Mauretania*.

Mauretania's final transatlantic crossing took place on 30th June 1934, the day before the official amalgamation of Cunard Line and White Star Line. After five cruises to the West Indies, her last sailing from New York was on 26th September 1934, the very day *Queen Mary* was launched. *Queen Mary* reclaimed the Blue Riband for Britain on her maiden voyage in May the following year.

At the end of a career spanning almost three decades, during which time she made 318 voyages including 54 cruises, *Mauretania* arrived at Southampton for the last time on 2nd October 1934. After disembarking her passengers and stores she was moved to Berth 108 on the far side of the new Southampton docks, her fate undecided.

The white *Mauretania*, above at Southampton and below in 1931 at New York. *(Top: Luis Miguel Correia Collection, bottom: J. & M. Clarkson collection]*

At the end of 1918 *Mauretania* made her first peacetime voyage from Southampton to New York shortly before Southampton became the home port for Cunard Line's express liners. Here she is shown in the early 1920s outbound for the United States. Note the large number of lifeboats compared with pre-war views of the ship. *[World Ship Society Collection]*

This 1931 stern view at New York clearly shows the second class promenade on B Deck with bulwarks instead of rails. *[J. & M. Clarkson Collection]*

A moody shot of her arrival at New York. *[Bob Bradshaw Collection]*

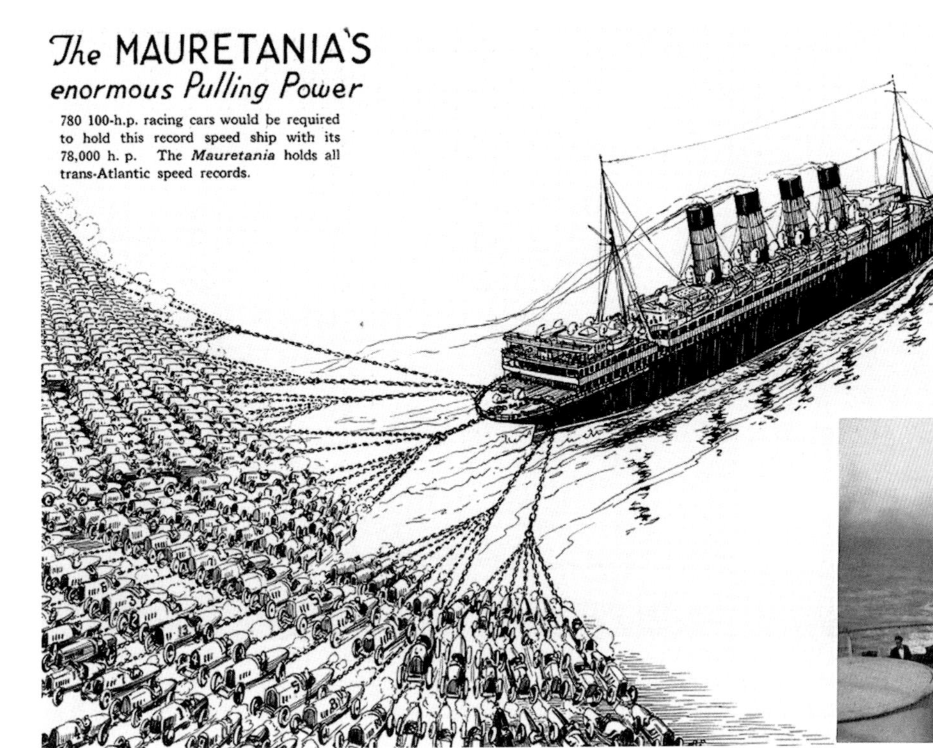

The MAURETANIA'S
enormous Pulling Power
780 100-h.p. racing cars would be required to hold this record speed ship with its 78,000 h. p. The *Mauretania* holds all trans-Atlantic speed records.

Despite the arrival of more advanced ships, *Mauretania*'s power was always impressive as this cartoon and unusual view of the wake of her quadruple screws clearly illustrates. [Left: *Ian Farquhar Collection;* below: *World Ship Society Collection]*

Mauretania returned to the Tyne on 11th September 1921 for conversion from coal to oil fuel burning. The work took almost five months to complete at a cost of a quarter of a million pounds. Not only was the workforce in the engine room reduced significantly, the environment was free of the coal dust which inevitably found its way into every nook and cranny. *[Top: Ian Rae Collection; left: Tyne and Wear Archives]*

Between November 1923 and May 1924 she underwent another major refit, this time to her turbines. At the same time, the forward end of the First Class Promenade was plated in and fitted with sliding windows. This can been seen in these two Southampton views. Above she is backing out of her berth in the Ocean Dock, with White Star Line's *Homeric* on the right and United States Line's *Leviathan* in front of her. In the far distance is the South Western Hotel. *[Above: Southern Daily Echo; below: World Ship Society Collection]*

Above: On 19th October 1932 *Mauretania* became the first ship to be berthed in Southampton's New Docks, which were built to the west of the old port. *[A. Andrews Collection]*
Below: Alongside the New Docks towards the end of her career as a transatlantic liner, with White Star Line's *Homeric* astern. The 20-inch overhang on the Boat and Promenade Decks is clearly shown. *[Paul Louden-Brown Collection]*

Almost 25 years after she was built, she was still able to produce speeds of around 27 knots. Here she is off the Spanish coast in May 1932 on the way to beating her own record from Gibraltar to Southampton. *[Peter Newall Collection]*

Why Not a Cruise This Winter?

Mauretania

The Blue Ribbon Ship of the Atlantic

***to the* Mediterranean**

From New York, February 7th, 1923

Swiftly, sumptuously across the Atlantic to the blue waters, sunny skies and glamoured shores of history, romance and story. Something entirely different from the usual Winter holidays. Something incomparable in pleasure, interest and personal benefit.

Cost compares favorably with average expenses of Wintering at home. Prices for entire cruise range from $950 up according to stateroom.

The name of every port of call stirs the imagination — brings vivid pictures to the mind's eye and inspires desire to go. Madeira, Gibraltar, Algiers, Monte Carlo, Italy (Rome and Naples), the Dardanelles, Constantinople, Greece (Athens, Eleusis, Marathon), Palestine, (Haifa, Jerusalem, Bethlehem, Nazareth, Tiberias, Damascus), Egypt (Cairo, Memphis and up the mystic Nile to Luxor, Karnak, Thebes, Assuan and the first cataract). Leisurely inland excursions, with every conceivable travel comfort are planned at all of them.

Mauretania to the Mediterranean is the luxury cruise this Winter, providing a degree of comfort and opportunities for shipboard entertainment never before attained in Mediterranean Cruises. It is under the well-known management of the Travel Department of the American Express Company in full cooperation with the Cunard Line. To insure ample choice of staterooms, reservation should be made NOW.

ALSO:

The Pacific Liner "Ebro" to SOUTH AMERICA

***68 days across and below the Equator.* From New York, Jan. 24, 1923**

Visiting the most interesting ports including Robinson Crusoe's Island — across the Andes Mountains, 8 days at Rio de Janeiro (Brazilian Centennial Exposition). $1190 and up. Also several special tours to the Brazilian Exposition up to February 17.

For full information, details, itinerary, etc., call at any American Express office or write direct to

American Express Travel Department

65 Broadway, New York, N. Y.

Wherever you travel always carry American Express Travelers Cheques

Left: *Mauretania* first operated as a cruise ship in February 1923 when she was chartered by American Express for an exclusive Mediterranean cruise from New York. Above she is seen boarding passengers by tender on one of her cruises. *[Both Peter Newall Collection]*

Below: Between April and September 1931 she offered weekend cruises during turnarounds in New York. These were priced from as little as $50 per person. *[Adam Gratwick Collection]*

In May 1933 *Mauretania* was converted into a full-time cruise ship. Painted white, her aft lifeboats were also removed because of the lower passenger capacity. *[World Ship Society Collection]*

Her first cruises in her new role were two back-to-back voyages from Southampton. Here she is at Madeira on the 13th June 1933, dwarfing Union-Castle Line's four-funnelled *Arundel Castle* (19,023/1921). *[Luis Miguel Correia Collection]*

This photo taken at Southampton by R. Snook on 9th June 1934 shows work being done on the dome of the Second Class Lounge. It also appears that the area along the First Class Boat Deck has been painted, possible green. At some stage she also had green boot-topping, the same as Cunard Line's *Franconia* and *Carinthia* when they operated as cruise ships. *[Fred Hawks Collection]*

Above left: Tying up in Southampton's New Docks. *[Michael Pocock Collection]*
Above right: A forlorn sight, laid up at Berth 108, Southampton. *[Peter Newall Collection]*

HAROLD PETO AND THE SEARCH FOR MAURETANIA'S INTERIOR DESIGNER

In March 1905 Cunard Line approached fifteen interior designers to submit designs for the first class interiors of the 'new fast steamers - No. 367 and 735'. Most of these, including George Trollope and Sons and S. J. Waring and Sons Ltd., had previously carried out work on passenger liners. The Glasgow architect James Miller (1860-1947), however, had never been involved in such a project but had produced designs for the Glasgow International Exhibition of 1901 and a number of important buildings in Glasgow. He was probably recommended by J.G. Dunlop, Managing Director of John Brown and Co. Ltd. or Cunard Line's Chairman, Lord Inverclyde, who also had an office at 20 Jamaica Street, Glasgow.

For one reason or another, with the exception of James Miller, most of the contenders for the contract fell by the wayside and the search continued for other designers. Lord Inverclyde apparently consulted the eminent architect and former head of the Royal Institute of British Architects Sir Aston Webb and another name was thrown into the hat, Harold Ainsworth Peto. Peto was certainly not an obvious choice but as Lord Inverclyde noted: 'He is now giving himself entirely to interior decoration and designing private houses and seems to do a great deal in this way, both in London, the country and abroad. Of course the whole idea of ship decoration is entirely new to him.'

Harold Peto as a young man.
[Robin Whalley Collection]

Harold Peto was born in 1854, the eighth out of fourteen children. His father Sir Samuel Morton Peto was a wealthy building contractor whose firm constructed many famous London landmarks including Nelson's Column and the Reform Club. Samuel later became involved with railway construction and was made a baronet in 1855. A Liberal Member of Parliament for Bristol, he was declared bankrupt in 1866 following the collapse of the Overend and Gurney Bank. Not only did he have to give up his seat in Parliament but he also had to sell his grand house in Suffolk, Somerleyton Hall. Despite his father's misfortunes, Harold was educated at Harrow and later trained as an architect. In 1874 he went into partnership with Ernest George. The practice was very successful and among the houses they designed was one for W.S. Gilbert of Gilbert and Sullivan fame. The famous architects Edwin Lutyens and Herbert Baker also started their careers working at George and Peto.

In 1892 because of Harold's disenchantment with the architectural styles of the day, the partnership was dissolved on condition that he did not practice architecture in England for a number of years. This was a major turning point in his career and his great knowledge and love of the Italian Renaissance led to frequent visits to Italy. He also turned his attention to garden design and over the following years built up a great reputation as a garden designer. His commissions included the gardens at Buscot Park, Oxfordshire, Ilnacullin Island, Ireland and a number of gardens and villas in the South of France. In 1899 he bought Iford Manor, a dilapidated Elizabethan house on the banks of the River Frome, near Bradford-on-Avon, Wiltshire. Here he transformed the grounds into one of the finest gardens in England. He also had a London residence at 9 Bryanston Square.

On 24th May 1905 Lord Inverclyde and Edward Cunard met with Harold Peto to discuss the interior decoration for the new ships. Edward Cunard was the grandson of Cunard Line's founder Samuel Cunard, and the last member of the Cunard family on the board. At this meeting Peto stressed that he would prefer to work with one or two directors rather than the entire Board because 'each would think that his taste was best.' It was agreed that he would visit *Lucania* and *Caronia* at Liverpool to understand more about ship decoration. He was also asked to submit designs for the decoration and furnishing of the first class public rooms on one of the new ships. His contract would include the supervision of the furnishing, electric lighting and ventilation of these rooms as well as fifty of the best first class staterooms. It was also stressed that: 'while they (the directors) wish everything connected with the designing and decorating of the First Class accommodation in their new ships to be of the best workmanship and material, they do not desire anything of an extravagant nature. The simpler the nature of the work, as long as it is good, the better, and the more the cost can be kept down...'

However, from the start there was a sticking point over Peto's proposed charges. Whilst Cunard wished him to be paid a fixed fee of £1,500 for his work, Peto, who had considerable experience in dealing with architectural payments, was adamant that he should be paid a commission of between 5% and 7.5% of the total costs. This was the usual method for paying architects and Peto knew that the highly detailed work would take up at least two years of his time. He also realized that, with such a large project, there would undoubtedly be numerous changes to designs and that the extra work would not be properly covered by a fixed fee.

During the next few months negotiation continued over the contract for *Mauretania*'s interior design. At one time in the proceedings Lord Inverclyde was inclined to drop Peto and find someone else. However, Edward Cunard continued to champion his use: 'I hear indirectly through a mutual friend that he was surprised at the small offer we made him, but nevertheless I know he is anxious to do the work but he has a feeling that it would be rather unprofessional and rather beneath his dignity to accept such a figure...I feel confident from what I have seen of Peto that he would make a success of the ship.' Eventually, on 13th September 1905, the terms of the contract were agreed. Peto would be paid a fee based on 5% of the total interior cost. This charge would not be more than £4,000 but would not be lower than £3,000. The project would include designing, drawing and supervision of the first class accommodation. The second class accommodation would be designed by the shipyard, with plans approved by Peto. The work would be overseen by a Clerk of the Works who would be appointed by Peto and based in Newcastle.

Using Peto's designs, the panelling and decoration for most of the first class accommodation was undertaken by two London West End contractors; W. Turner Lord and Company and Charles Mellier and Company. On 5th June 1906 the former agreed to undertake the following work: Grand Staircase £15,768, Lower Dining Saloon £12,979, à la carte restaurant £4,251 and the Smoke Room £7,276, totalling £40,274. The total amount later increased to almost £49,000 and the work was completed in July 1907. Mellier was responsible for a number of the first class cabins, the Lounge and Library and Writing Room. This cost just over £17,300 and the work was finished in March 1907.

Meanwhile in Glasgow, James Miller, *Lusitania*'s architect, agreed to far less favourable terms than Harold Peto. He was employed in an advisory capacity, with John Brown and Co. Ltd. producing all the drawings based on his ideas. For this work he was paid a fee of only £1,000. The result of these different approaches is evident in the overall interior designs for the two ships. Peto's meticulous involvement in the design is to be found throughout *Mauretania*. His attention to detail was quite remarkable with small features such as a crossed ribbon pattern occurring not only on cabin door furniture but also in columns in the main public rooms. There is also a greater sense of harmony as one moves from one space to the next. Although *Lusitania*'s interiors were undoubtedly attractive, there appears to be less cohesion in her overall design.

On Harold Peto's death in 1933 his papers were left to a relative in Bristol and it is believed that they were destroyed in a bombing raid in the city during the Second World War. Regrettably, these probably included his drawings for *Mauretania* as none have come to light during the research for this book.

The beautiful Iford Manor from the banks of the River Frome bought by Harold Peto in 1899 in a dilapidated condition.

The grounds were tansformed into one of the finest gardens in England. With its classical features, the Great Terrace at Iford Manor on a hot summer's day is like being in a villa in Tuscany.

PASSENGER ACCOMODATION

First Class, also known as Saloon

At the time of their completion, Cunard Line claimed that *Mauretania* and *Lusitania* offered fifty percent more light and air space and deck promenade per passenger than any other liner afloat. The accommodation for the 563 (589 from 1922) first class passengers aboard *Mauretania* was indeed spacious. These were offset by an attractive green stair carpet.

In the Grand Staircase stairwell were two electric passenger elevators, each operated by a lift attendant. The elevator cages were also panelled in walnut whilst the ornate grille surrounding the elevator was made from aluminium. The use of this metal instead of iron or bronze was unusual for that time and produced a weight saving of some 20 tons. The lift mechanism and steel cable were also cleverly hidden from view, with the main pulley for each elevator situated above the wrought-iron domed skylight on A Deck. The cable then continued across the top of the dome of the First Class Library and Writing Room to a winding drum and balance weight. The latter travelled in a five deck-high trunkway, which also acted as a ventilator.

Grand Staircase and entrance halls

First class accommodation occupied much of amidships and was spread over five decks: D Deck; C Deck; Upper C Deck; B Deck and A Deck. These were also known technically as Main, Upper, Shelter, Promenade and Boat Decks.

The main access between these decks was via the Grand Staircase, the design of which was based on the Italian Renaissance 15th century period, and consisted of figured French walnut panelling and woodwork. Here the subtlety and detail of Harold Peto's design is most evident. Simplicity was the key, with flat pilasters, topped by carved capitals, flanking large quartered veneer panels of the finest quality.

At each deck level, the foyer or so-called Grand Entrance was also treated in a relatively uncomplicated but elegant manner. The floors were covered in white India rubber tiles with small black squares, whilst the white painted enamel wood ceilings had octagonal and shaped panels framed in flat mouldings, carved with wreaths and scrolls. There was also a variety of unusual columns and pilasters. The recessed settees facing the passenger lifts on A and Upper C Decks had especially fine carving. These comfortable seats had large cushions and were covered in the finest material. During one of the post-war refits, the A Deck settee was replaced by a glass-fronted kiosk.

A Deck Grand Entrance looking forward towards the Grand Staircase and elevator. *[Zogolovitch Collection]*

Facing aft. The recessed settee with the entrance to the Lounge on the left. *[Zogolovitch Collection]*

Two of the foyers were used as entrance halls for First Class passengers who entered the ship either through a pair of double watertight doors on D Deck or the main gangway on Upper C Deck. The latter tended to be used when boarding at the Liverpool Landing Stage or New York. The Purser's Bureau on B Deck was also panelled in walnut, using the same design features as the Grand Staircase. Like the elevator grille work, the fancy grille above the Bureau counter was made from aluminium.

The main rendezvous point or lobby for the first class public rooms was the Grand Entrance hallway on A Deck with its wicker chairs and numerous potted plants. From here, passengers could also reach the Boat Deck Promenade, via a weatherproofed vestibule. The exposed promenade wrapped around the A Deck housing and passengers were able to enjoy a bracing, if not windswept, walk around the ship.

All the woodwork and decoration of the Grand Staircase and entrance halls was subcontracted to W. Turner Lord and Company, 120 Mount Street, London.

First Class Library and Writing Room

A major challenge in the design of the first class public rooms on A Deck was fitting these around four funnel uptakes and numerous boiler room vents, without spoiling their symmetry or impact. The Library and Writing Room, for example, had to be squeezed between the second funnel hatch, the Grand Entrance hallway and the third funnel hatch. Unlike the other rooms, which were orientated fore and aft, this chamber ran from port to starboard and with its oval-shaped glass dome, white marble fireplace and red curtains, was probably the most elegant of all the first class public rooms. The crimson and green trellis pattern carpet was by Wilton, whilst the style of the woodwork, columns and furniture was based on neo-classical late 18th century French designs. The panelling was described in contemporary literature as being of sycamore stained silver grey although later photographs show panels which are darker in colour. Sycamore was often stained to look like harewood. The detailed gilt carving was exquisite not only on the freestanding columns but also the panels surrounding the bookcases. The bookcases had diamond shaped brass grilles in the door panels and were copied from the Trianon Library at Versailles.

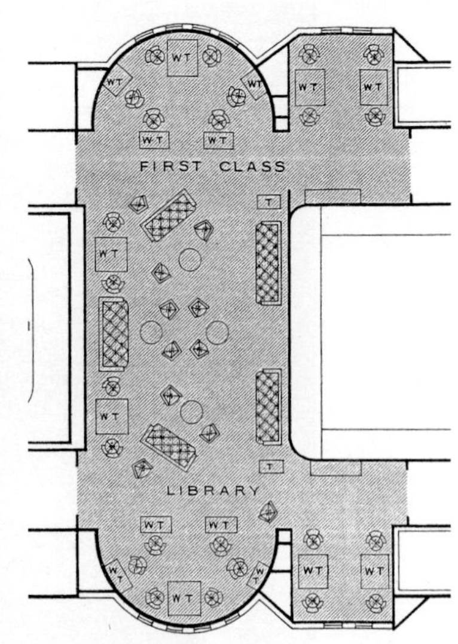

The swing doors to the Library and Writing Room were each fitted with a dozen bevelled, plate glass panes. These gave a virtually uninterrupted view aft for almost 350 feet on both sides of the ship. On the port and starboard ends of the library were bay windows with sea views. The room also had numerous mahogany writing tables with leather holders containing writing paper and envelopes.

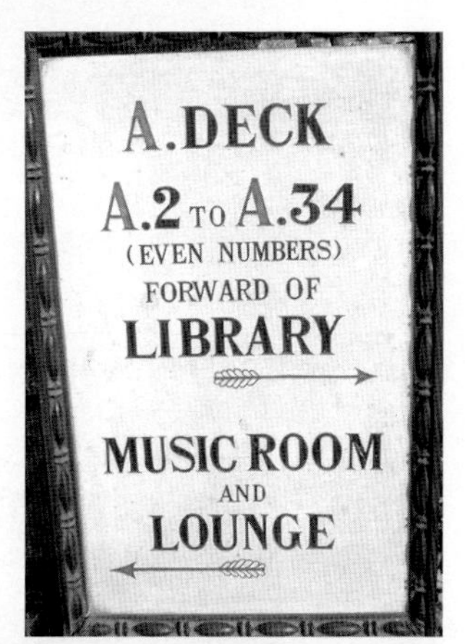

Two port views of the Library, one with the curtains open and one closed. *[Top: Zogolovitch Collection; bottom: Paul Louden-Brown Collection]*

First Class Lounge

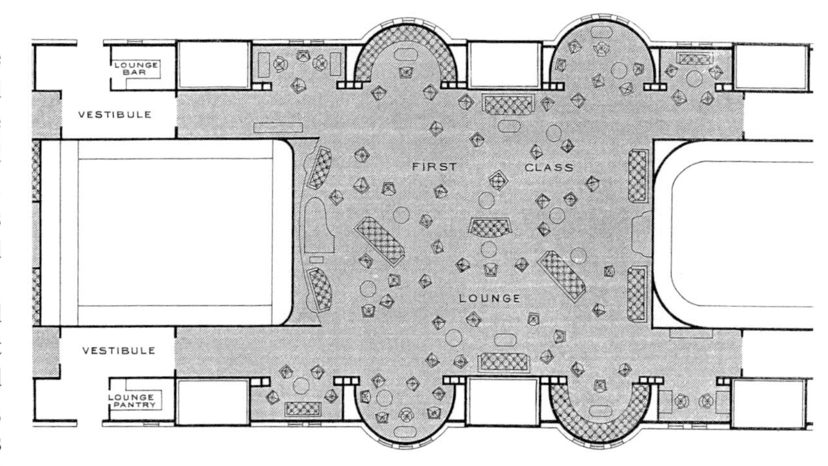

Aft of the Grand Entrance hallway was the magnificent First Class Lounge, which was situated between the third and fourth funnel hatches. Like the Library and Writing Room, this room also used designs from the late 18th century French period. All the furniture and decoration in these two rooms was subcontracted to the London decorators and cabinetmakers, Charles Mellier and Company.

Also known as the Music Room and Lounge, this chamber was 80 feet long by 56 feet wide. Most of the woodwork was dull polished mahogany with beautifully carved fluted columns, each culminating in an ornate gilt capital with ram's heads, swags and the profile of a lady. The carpet was manufactured by Wilton and had a large green leaf trellis and blush pink rose pattern whilst specially woven Aubusson tapestries lined three sides of the room. There were also bronze and cut crystal electrically-lit ceiling lights and a mantelpiece and 16 pilasters made from lilac coloured *fleur de pêche* marble. The room had a sense of elegance, but which was not overbearing. The whole was surmounted by a large 18-foot diameter glass dome, which let in natural light.

Comfortable French-style, floral-patterned settees and chairs were dotted around the lounge whilst, on the port and starboard side, a pair of bay windows, lined with silk curtains, provided cosy alcoves for passengers to enjoy private conversation. With a grand piano at the aft end, the room was also the venue for concerts by the ship's orchestra. In the 1922 Tyne refit, a new parquet dance floor was laid and after that time, the lounge was sometimes referred to as the Ballroom. Prior to that, dancing took place in the Dining Saloon on C Deck.

The Lounge as built, looking forward. Note the marble pilasters and tapestries. *[Zogolovitch Collection]*

In the 1920s many of the public rooms, including the Lounge, featured large ornamental palms. *[Peter Newall Collection]*

In 1922 a new parquet floor was fitted and in the evenings the Lounge became a ballroom. *[World Ship Society Collection]*

First Class Smoke Room

Beyond the lounge was that essentially male preserve, the Smoke Room. It was reached via a walnut-panelled corridor or vestibule, which ran either side of the fourth funnel hatching. The vestibule also had outer doors, which opened onto the Boat Deck promenade.

Because of the position of large engine room ventilators in the centre and on the port and starboard sides, the layout of the 53-feet long by 50-feet wide Smoke Room was cleverly divided into two spaces, with a panelled screen separating each chamber. Along the entire length ran a wagon-vaulted glass and enamelled-wood ceiling with a carved frieze of shells, vases, swags and other ornamental motifs. Like the Grand Staircase and entrance halls, the style of the Smoke Room was based on 15th century Italian Renaissance designs. Produced by the same contractor, W. Turner Lord and Company, the decoration was, however, more ornate.

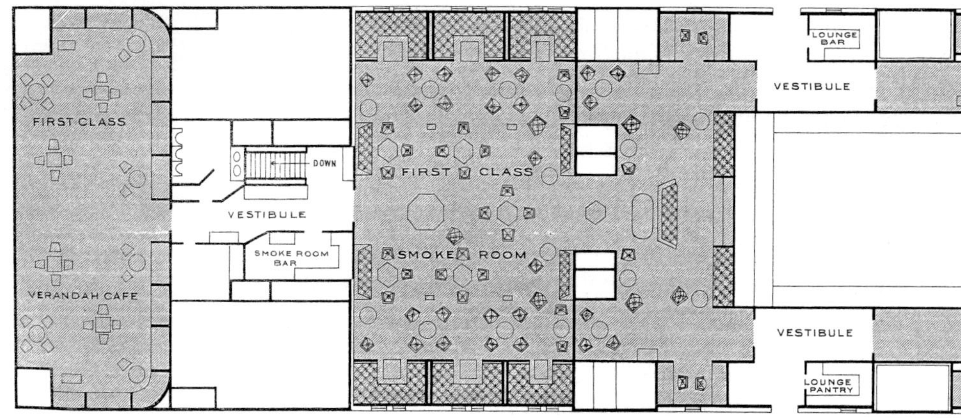

The aft part of the Smoke Room, looking through the partition at the hooded fireplace. Note the octagonal-shaped table, which was used for the daily sweepstake. *[Zogolovitch Collection]*

French walnut was used throughout the room. Its soft colouring gave a more relaxed and sophisticated ambience than the traditional dark and heavy masculine atmosphere of smoke rooms of the period. The magnificent walnut veneered panels also had inlaid chain pattern borders of sycamore. This pattern was repeated in the lower part of the swing doors leading aft. These doors were notable for their glazed colonnaded panels and intricate chased brass handles.

At the forward end of the Smoke Room the focal point was a large open fireplace lined with green marble. The carved hood featured the fish scale pattern found on many of the columns and pilasters in the Smoke Room and Grand Staircase. In 1907, it was claimed that the carved walnut fireplace was based on one by the Italian sculptor Della Robbia in the Victoria and Albert Museum, South Kensington, London. In fact, only the design of the angels in the centre came from a fireplace in the Victoria and Albert and that was made in Florence around 1455-58 by Geri da Settignano.

Above the fireplace was a lunette-shaped oil painting by Frank Stuart Murray entitled 'Old Liverpool'. A companion painting 'Old New York' was at the aft end of the vaulted roof.

Recesses, partitioned by finely carved turned columns, were on either side of the Smoke Room. In the forward space there were two double writing recesses with desks and paper racks, offering complete privacy. In the main room comfortable, shaped divans filled the three recesses on each side. Natural light flowed in from the glass ceiling and 14 large arched sliding windows. In the centre of the room stood a large, solid walnut octagonal-shaped table. This was used for the sale of sweepstake tickets for the ship's daily run. Eminent passengers acted as auctioneers, and the table was marked with thousands of hammer blows from the auctioneer's gavel.

Top: The distinctive fireplace. *[Tyne & Wear Archives]*
Middle: Facing aft in the forward chamber. *[Peter Newall Collection]*
Below: The double doors in the Smoke Room led to the Verandah Café. Above these was the painting *Old New York. [Peter Newall Collection]*

Verandah Café

A pair of swing doors led from the Smoke Room to a walnut panelled vestibule, the Smoke Room Bar, and the aft staircase with its mahogany handrails and balusters. At the end of the vestibule doors opened onto the Verandah Café. Here passengers could take tea or a drink and enjoy the sea air and the view to the stern. However, compared with the opulence in other areas of the first class accomodation, the Verandah Café was relatively plain with unadorned chairs, benches, side windows and skylight. Although it was protected from the weather on two sides, it was probably quite uncomfortable in a following wind.

In the 1927 refit it was remodelled along the lines of the Orangery at Hampton Court Palace. Panels were added to the aft end whilst all the walls had green painted wood trelliswork attached. The plain columns were also encased in wood columns with Ionic capitals. Wicker furniture replaced the chairs and benches. The whole area was centrally heated and part of the deck was specially treated for dancing. During cruises, the Verandah Café was a popular place to visit, especially as it overlooked the specially constructed 18 foot by 15 foot, 5 foot 6 inches deep, wood-framed swimming pool on A Deck aft.

During the 1910s and 1920s, winter gardens aboard transatlantic liners became the vogue. After its transformation in 1927, the Verandah Café was filled with a variety of plants including azaleas, hyacinths, cyclamen, chrysanthemums, ferns and potted bay trees. These were carefully tended by the ship's gardener. The gardener also looked after the numerous plants in the first class entrance halls and the large palms, which were placed at the centres of the First Class Lounge, Library and Writing Room and Dining Saloon. Although the overall effects of these plants was to give the ship the feel of being in a great English country house, the positioning of the palms spoiled the symmetry of the rooms. Harold Peto, the consummate gardener, would probably not have approved of these in his carefully designed chambers.

The Verandah Café as built and after the 1927 refit. *[Top: Zogolovitch Collection; left: Paul Louden-Brown Collection]*

First class passengers wishing to enjoy the sea air could walk around the ship along the exposed promenade on A Deck.
[Ambrose Greenway Collection]

First Class Dining Saloon

More evidence of French style was to be found in one of the most impressive rooms on the ship, the three deck-high First Class Dining Saloon, situated between the third and fourth funnel hatches on C and Upper C Decks. The style of this room and its magnificent dome was from the reign of François I (1515-1547), France's first Renaissance king. A great patron of the arts, François I employed many famous Italian Renaissance artists. The designs of the period were an interesting combination of late Gothic and classical Italian Renaissance.

The lower Dining Saloon on C Deck was 87 feet long and extended the full width of the ship. It had seating for 328 passengers. In the centre was an octagonal, balustraded opening to the upper part of the Dining Saloon on Upper C Deck. This area featured an intimate à la carte restaurant for 142 passengers. Thus, almost all first class passengers could be fed in a single sitting. The galleys for both first and second class were aft of the lower Dining Saloon and food was transferred between the two First Class Dining Saloons in a service lift.

The wood chosen for the Dining Saloon was light-coloured weathered oak. This gave a gentle warm glow to the room, which was lit by hidden electric lighting in the dome and by natural light from pairs of portholes on the lower level and on the upper level by windows overlooking the Upper C Deck promenade. The decoration on the lower level was more ornate than the upper saloon and consisted mainly of arched panels richly carved with various classical motifs such as cornucopias, vases, dolphin heads, and shields. No two adjoining panels had the same design. The room was also partially divided by arched panels with mirrors, which ran at right angles from the ship's side to enclosed ventilator shafts. The upholstery was deep pink whilst the carpet was cerise red. W. Turner Lord and Company undertook all the work in this room.

Aboard *Mauretania* traditional long tables in the First Class Dining Saloon made way for a range of table sizes seating from five to fourteen passengers per table in the lower saloon and from two to six in the upper saloon. In the post-war period the variety of table sizes was increased considerably whilst dining chairs replaced the old-fashioned, fixed, armless swivel chairs. Before the First Class Lounge became a ballroom, the chairs and tables in the centre of the lower dining saloon were unbolted after dinner and passengers danced on the parquet floor to music from the ship's small orchestra.

Top: The full glory of the Dining Saloon. *[Zogolovitch Collection]*

The crowning feature of the First Class Dining Saloon was a white and gold groined plaster dome. This was on B Deck, and at the junctures of the groins were plaques with signs of the Zodiac. The centre of the dome culminated in an octagonal balustrated opening mirroring the one below.

Towards the end of *Mauretania*'s career, part of the lower dining room became a cinema. 'Talkies' were introduced on the ship soon after she returned to her peacetime duties in 1919. During cruises, movies were shown and in a 1931 cruise deck plan the Second Class Saloon was also labelled the Motion Picture Saloon. As many of her cruises operated as a one-class ship, movies were probably shown here after dinner.

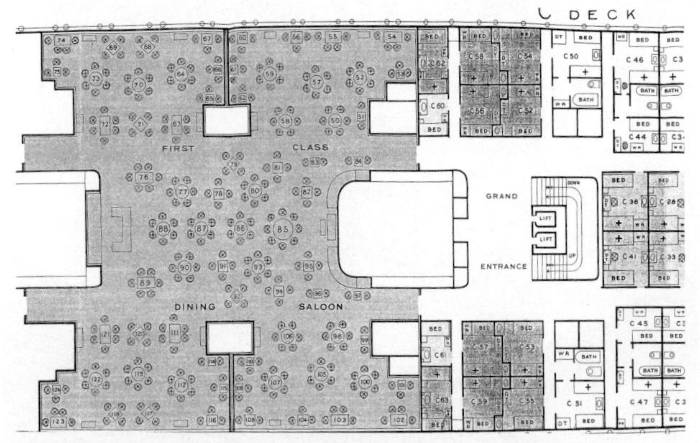

Lower Dining Saloon

Middle: The 328 passengers who used the lower Dining Saloon ate from a set menu. This pre-war illustration shows various activities in first class, including lunch in the main Dining Saloon. *[Zogolovitch Collection]*

Bottom: In the 1920s dining chairs and smaller tables replaced the old-fashioned fixed armless swivel chairs and large tables. *[Paul Louden-Brown Collection]*

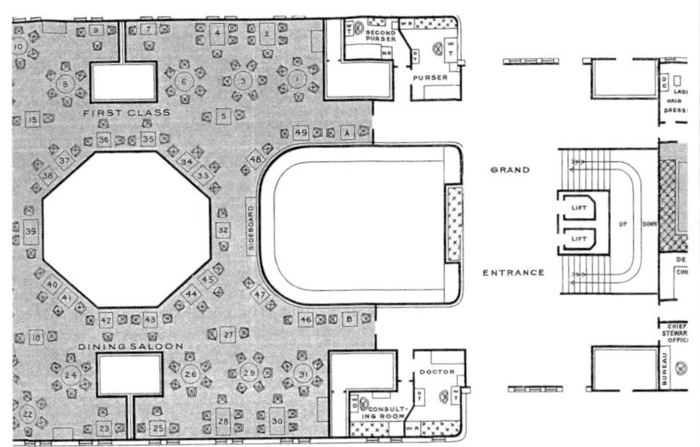

Upper Dining Saloon

The upper Dining Saloon was a smaller à la carte restaurant for 142 passengers. This advertisement (right) for Colman's Mustard gives a good idea of the sense of occasion in this Dining Saloon.
[Right: Paul Louden-Brown Collection; bottom: Zogolovitch Collection]

THE
"MAURETANIA"
AND
COLMAN'S D.S.F. MUSTARD.
BULL'S HEAD
How perfect everything is here! I see the mustard is Colman's.
Colman's Mustard follows the flag and maintains the record for British reliability and perfection. Accept no substitute.

R.M.S. "MAURETANIA."

Wednesday, September 29th, 1909

MENU.

Cantaloupe
Hors d'Œuvres — Varies

Petite Marmite | Potage St. Germain

Brill—Parsley Sauce | Fried Fillets of Sole—Tartare

Braized Sweetbreads—Financiere | Venison Cutlets—Oporto

Sirloin and Ribs of Beef | Saddle of Southdown Mutton
Roast Young Turkey | Bradenham Ham

Kidney Beans | Rice | Braized Onions
Garfield and Boiled Potatoes

Aylesbury Ducklings

Pouding Berkeley
Apple Tart | Gelee au Marasquin
Gateau Cunard
French Ice Cream and Wafers

Dessert

Tea | Coffee

Blue Ribbon of the Atlantic.

R.M.S. "MAURETANIA."

Friday February 5th, 1909

MENU

Hors d'Œuvres—Varies
Bluepoints

Chicken Gombo | Potage St. Germain

Halibut—Caper Sauce | Salmon Trout—Creole

Lamb Cutlets — Renaissance | Jugged Hare — Francaise

Haunch of Venison—Port Wine Sauce
Roast Sirloin and Ribs of Beef | Boiled Turkey—Celery Sauce
Ox Tongue—Spinach

Peas | Rice | Grilled Mushrooms
Boiled and Roast Potatoes

Celery Fed Duckling

Pouding Coburg
Pumpkin Pie | Bavaroise Ananas | Savoie Biscuit Glacé

French Ice Cream and Wafers

Dessert

Tea | Coffee

Choice of Cold Meats.

The 20 or so years which separate these first class transatlantic menus show how much taste had changed from the rather stodgy and relatively limited Edwardian cuisine to the variety of choice in the 1920s. *[Above: John Avery Collection; bottom: Zogolovitch Collection]*

: CARTE DU JOUR :

R.M.S. "MAURETANIA."

FRIDAY, SEPTEMBER 28, 1928

DINNER

TO ORDER

HORS D'ŒUVRE

Oysters on the Half Shell | Caviar
Mayfair Clam Juice Cocktails | Grape Fruit Cocktails
Sprats in Oil | Œufs farcis aux Anchois | Salted Almonds
Salade d'Anchois | Salted Peanuts | Cantaloup Glace
Tomates a la Russe | Oreille de Veau Vinaigrette
Croutes Lucullus | Jambon Epicure | Canapes Danois
Matjes Herrings | Langue Ravigote | Smoked Salmon
Olives—Plain, Stuffed and Ripe

POTAGE

Consomme Paysanne | Onion Soup | Potage St. Germain
Consomme Perle | Creme Freneuse | Potage a l'Oseil

POISSON

Brook Trout Grenobloise | Salmon Hollandaise
Supreme of Sole Normande | Fried Smelts Tartare

ENTREE

Lamb Cutlets Tourangelle | Pintade Bonne Femme
Escalope de Foie Gras a la Gelee | Frog's Legs Meuniere
Filet Mignon aux Cepes | Saddle of Hare Poivrade

GRILL

Spring Chicken & Bacon | Mutton Cutlets Saratogas
Sirloin Steaks Maitre d'Hotel | Lamb Chops & Tomatoes

JOINTS

Roast Spring Lamb, Mint Sauce
Braised Cumberland Ham, Sauce Porto

ROAST

Roast Chicken, Bread Sauce
Duckling | Grain | Pigeon | Quail | Reine
Guinea Chicken | Partridge | Grouse | Teal Duck

CARNIVAL DINNER.

READY DISHES

HORS D'ŒUVRE VARIE
CONSOMME PAYSANNE | POTAGE ST. GERMAIN
ROAST SPRING LAMB, MINT SAUCE
BRAISED CUMBERLAND HAM, SAUCE PORTO
VEGETABLES | POTATOES
ROAST CHICKEN, BREAD SAUCE
SALAD
SWEETS | ICE CREAM
FRUIT | COFFEE

TO ORDER

VEGETABLES

Artichokes, Sauce Mousseline | Parsnips Maitre d'Hotel
String Beans au Beurre | Spinach a la Creme
Potatoes—Boiled | Mashed | Anna | Chateau
Saratoga | Croquette | Creamed | French Fried

SALADS

Lettuce | Chicory | Rachel | Cold Slaw
Ninon | Potato | Nicoise | Waldorf

SWEET

Pouding Souffle Rothschild
Compote de Fruits | Fresh Plum Flan | Ananas Carmelite
Choux a la Creme | Shortcake aux Bananes
Petits Fours | Patisserie Francaise
Sorbet a l'Ananas

ICES | Vanilla | Neapolitan | Nougat Parfait
Coupes Comtesse

SAVOURY

Laitance sur Toast | Manx Canapes | Devils on Horseback
Croutes au Fromage | Pailles au Parmesan

Dessert | Cafe

It will facilitate the service if orders are given in advance to the Waiter, and alternatively there is a small variety of Dishes already prepared as shown.

First class staterooms

As built, *Mauretania* had 253 first class staterooms. The variety on offer was considerable, not only in terms of numbers of passengers per cabin, but also in design. There were 35 single-berth rooms, 126 doubles and 92 three-berth rooms, spread over four decks: 48 on D Deck, 62 on C Deck, 110 on B Deck and 33 on A Deck. No staterooms were situated on Upper C Deck.

The finest accommodation was to be found on B Deck with its promenade deck running aft of the second funnel hatching. Unlike that on *Lusitania*, this promenade deck and the one on the deck above were 20 inches wider than Upper C Deck. This overhang provided first class passengers with slightly more deck space. In the 1924 refit the B Deck Promenade was partially plated in with large sliding windows.

On each side of the forward ends of the B Deck promenade were the Regal Suites. These magnificent rooms consisted of a drawing room or parlour, dining room for six, two bedrooms, bathroom and doors, which opened onto the main corridor or the promenade deck. The port side suite was panelled mainly in satinwood whilst the other featured Italian walnut panels. The walls were covered in silk and the overall design, like most of the interiors of the ship, was one of understated elegance.

Overlooking the B Deck Promenade were eight Parlour Suites, four on each side. These had en-suite bath and toilet facilities, a drawing room and separate bedroom. On B and A Deck, there were other en-suite staterooms and so-called Special Staterooms. Many of these 68 rooms were decorated by W. Turner Lord and Co. and featured a variety of styles from Adam to Sheraton. All had brass bedsteads and marble wash basins.

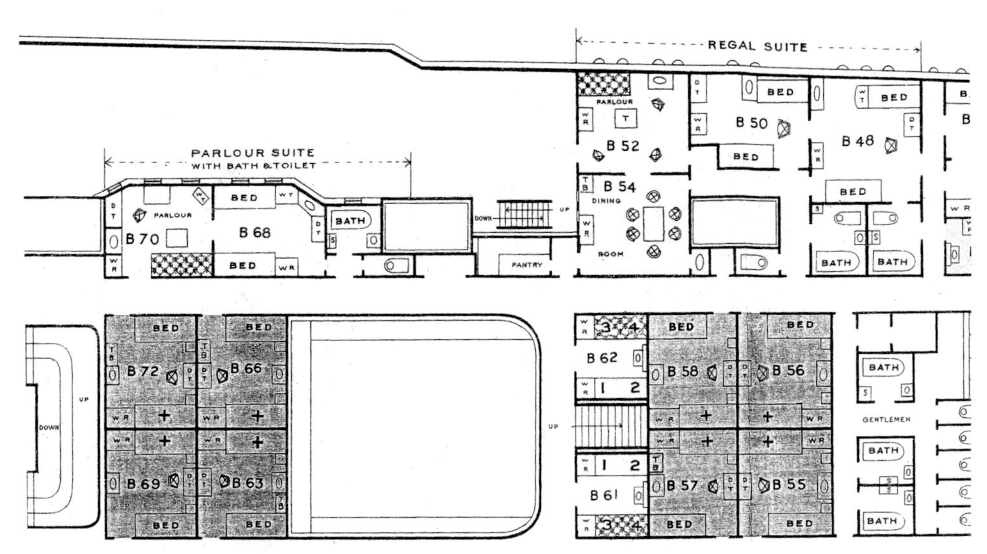

Port side promenade B Deck.

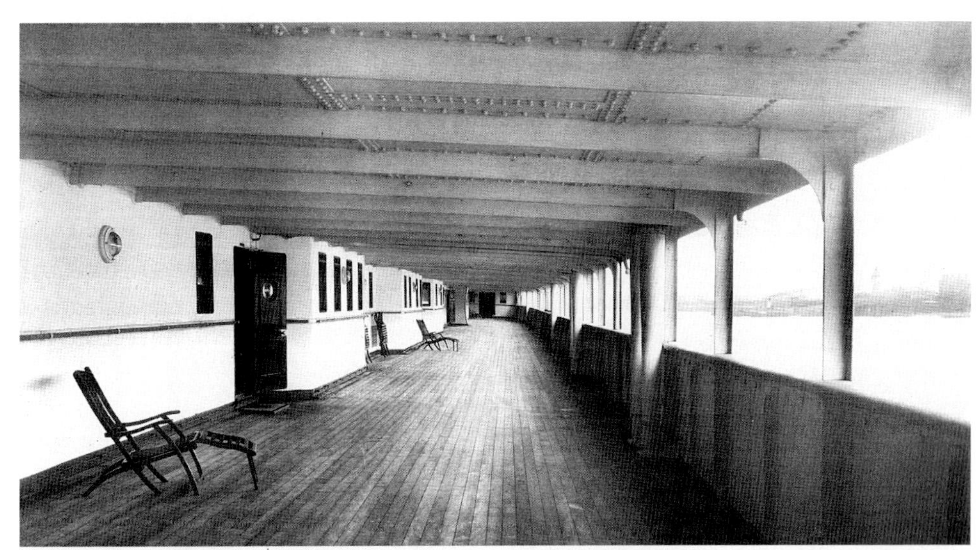

Middle: Starboard side promenade on B Deck facing forward towards the deck entrance of the Regal Suite.
Bottom: The private Dining Room in the starboard side Regal Suite had a marble fireplace and figured walnut panels. *(Both: Zogolovitch Collection]*

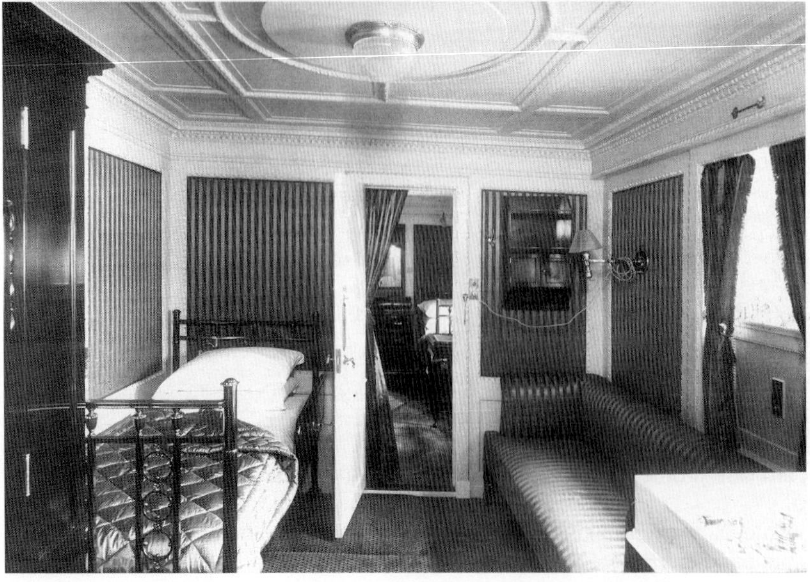

At the forward end of the B Deck first class accommodation was a semi-circular Observation Room with portholes overlooking the forecastle. Here passengers could stand and watch as the ship ploughed through the waves of the North Atlantic. During one of her post-war refits, most likely in 1921/1922, this space was filled in with bathrooms and two extra cabins, one of which was for bank staff.

Improvements in en-suite facilities were also made throughout the 1920s, especially after the 1921 fire in which most of the D Deck first class staterooms beneath the Lower Dining Saloon were severely damaged. In the 1927 refit 100 staterooms were refurbished, many of them on B Deck. Some of the outer rooms were enlarged whilst many of the inner staterooms were converted from double to single bed cabins.

Mauretania and *Lusitania* were also the first liners to be fitted with an extensive telephone system, which was connected to the New York and Liverpool telephone exchanges when alongside in these two ports. Receivers were installed in the best first class cabins enabling these passengers to stay in touch with the outside world whilst in port and also with each other during the sea voyage.

Top: The walls and seating in the parlour or drawing room in the port side Regal Suite were covered in green-striped silk.
Middle: The same pattern of silk was used in the bedrooms.
Bottom: A bedroom in one of the Parlour Suites. *[Top: Kay and Roy Cope Collection; middle and bottom: Zogolovitch Collection]*

Other first class facilities

For the few children who travelled first class aboard *Mauretania*, there was a Children's Dining Saloon and Nursery forward of the Grand Entrance on Upper C Deck. Here children were able to take their meals and play under the supervision of four stewardesses and two matrons. The mahogany and white enamelled walls were decorated with five paintings by the Newcastle-on-Tyne artist J.E. Mitchell illustrating the nursery rhyme 'Four and twenty blackbirds'. This area was later reduced in size after the installation of a ladies hairdresser and a gentleman's barber shop. The doctor's consulting room was also on Upper C Deck.

On the starboard side of the A Deck Grand Entrance hallway was a bookstall. In 1920 this became a branch of the London City and Midland Bank (renamed Midland Bank in 1923) whilst on the port side was the wireless office for sending and receiving telegrams.

Mauretania was completed just before the introduction of regular sports facilities aboard liners. There was no gymnasium or swimming pool and limited space for deck games. In many ways, that was part of her charm as she was one of the last of the 'floating country houses' on the Atlantic. However, in her latter years as a full time cruise ship, a wooden swimming pool was constructed on A Deck, just forward of the Second Class Lounge. Deck games and boxing matches were also held in the small open deck space between the first and second funnels. In the evenings after the war, movies were shown and passengers danced in the Lounge to music from the ship's orchestra or listened to 'wireless concerts'.

Top: The Children's Room on Upper C Deck. *[Zogolovitch Collection]*
Bottom: In the early 1920s *Mauretania* became the first Atlantic liner to be fitted with equipment to receive 'wireless concerts', which were listened to in the Lounge. *[Bob Bradshaw Collection]*

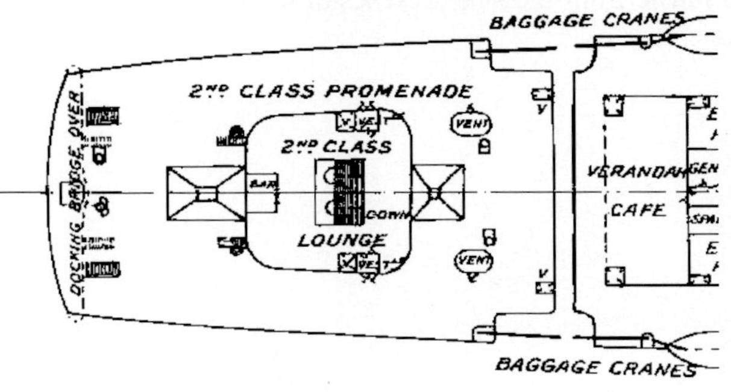

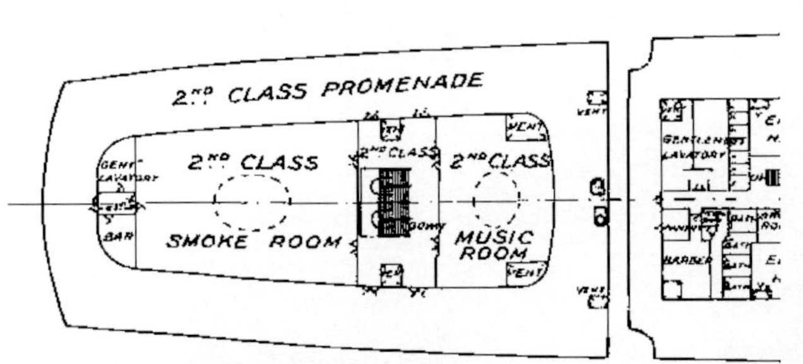

Second Class, also known as Second Cabin (Tourist Class from 1931)

The accommodation for the 475 passengers in second class (392 from 1922) was situated in the stern area abaft the main mast. Like first class, it was spread over five decks: D Deck; C Deck; Upper C Deck; B Deck and A Deck. These were also known as Main, Upper, Shelter, Promenade and Boat Decks. Access to the various decks was via a main staircase made from teak. The entrance halls also had white India rubber floor tiles with small black squares whilst the main boarding points were the same as first class, i.e. through a pair of double watertight doors on D Deck or the main gangway on Upper C Deck.

Although less sumptuous than first class, the accommodation in second class was a great improvement on earlier Cunard liners. Designed and made by the shipyard, under the supervision of Harold Peto, the public rooms had considerable charm. The Lounge on A Deck was at the head of the main staircase. Teak panelled, it was designed in the style of the late 18th century. Natural light entered the room through a circular glass dome and Venetian windows. The latter consisted of three windows, the central one being larger, with an arched top.

An early view of the second class promenade on A Deck showing the dome and triple windows of the Lounge. *[Bob Bradshaw Collection]*

Lounge and main staircase. *[Zogolovitch Collection]*

On B Deck were the Smoke Room and Drawing Room. The Smoke Room was aft of the entrance lobby. Also, featuring the late Georgian period, it was a traditional smoke room with mahogany panels, inlaid with English boxwood and burr mahogany, oval dome and windows. Forward of the entrance lobby was the Music Room or Drawing Room with its honey coloured maple panelling with gold swags and decoration. The piano was also made from maple. This comfortable retreat for ladies was based on 18th century French designs and had a domed roof.

Above: Entrance to the Smoke Room. *[Zogolovitch Collection]*

Left: A corner of the Drawing (Music) Room. *[Peter Newall Collection]*

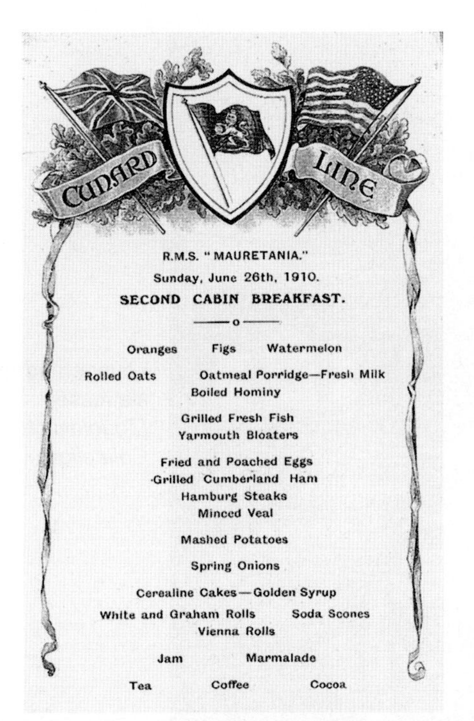
CUNARD LINE

R.M.S. "MAURETANIA."
Sunday, June 26th, 1910.
SECOND CABIN BREAKFAST.

o

Oranges Figs Watermelon

Rolled Oats Oatmeal Porridge—Fresh Milk
Boiled Hominy

Grilled Fresh Fish
Yarmouth Bloaters

Fried and Poached Eggs
Grilled Cumberland Ham
Hamburg Steaks
Minced Veal

Mashed Potatoes

Spring Onions

Cerealine Cakes—Golden Syrup

White and Graham Rolls Soda Scones
Vienna Rolls

Jam Marmalade

Tea Coffee Cocoa

The Dining Saloon was on C Deck. This fine room was 61 feet long and extended the full width of the ship. The style was again late 18th century and consisted of large carved panels of light oak. An octagonal opening into Upper C Deck formed a dome illuminated by electric lighting. The saloon could seat 250 passengers, mainly at long refectory tables. After the war these tables were replaced with a variety of smaller-size tables.

There were 133 second class staterooms situated on Upper C, C and D Decks. 34 were two berth cabins whilst the remainder had four berths. They were finished with white enamel panels, red carpets and soft wool taffeta hangings. A few of the superior staterooms on Upper C Deck were also fitted with large square windows instead of portholes.

An open promenade for second class passengers was on A Deck, whilst a covered promenade could be found on the deck below. The latter originally had open rails but sometime before the war these were replaced with bulwarks on the starboard and port sides. Later, the stern area was also given bulwarks.

Top: Second cabin breakfast menu. *[Bob Bradshaw Collection]*
Middle: The Dining Saloon in the 1920s.
[Paul Louden-Brown Collection]
Bottom: Even a four-berth cabin in second class was spacious and well furnished. The wash stand features a compactum or folding wash basin which was filled and emptied by the cabin steward. *[Zogolovitch Collection]*

Third Class (Tourist Third Cabin from the mid-1920s)

At the other end of the scale, the cabins for the 1,138 third class passengers were situated forward on D and E Decks. Although most of the 278 cabins were four berth, there were also 22 six-berth and 10 eight-berth cabins.

For most transatlantic lines in the early 20th century, third class emigrants provided the most profitable group of passengers carried. Every effort was made to ensure that these passengers received the best facilities for their fare, and aboard *Mauretania* Third Class had excellent accommodation. However, because it was at the forward end of the ship, it would have been quite uncomfortable at speed and during rough weather.

The Dining Saloon on C Deck was very spacious and could seat 330 people. It was panelled in polished ash with teak mouldings and had a piano at one end. During her cruising days, part of the saloon was partitioned to form a cinema.

A staircase led up from the Dining Saloon to the Smoke Room and General Room on Upper C Deck. The Smoke Room was on the port side whilst the General or Ladies Room was on the starboard side. Both rooms had polished ash panels. Also on Upper C Deck was the covered third class promenade which ran on either side for 320 feet. Part of this was plated in whilst some 180 feet on each side had open rails.

In 1922, following the reduction in the quota of emigrants allowed into the United States, the third class capacity on *Mauretania* was reduced to 767. It also became known as Tourist Third Cabin and attracted an entirely new market i.e. young travellers or students who wished to see Europe but at a low fare in reasonable accommodation.

Left: The Dining Saloon extended the whole width of the ship. *[Zogolovitch Collection]*
Bottom left: This four-berth cabin was basic but comfortable and a great improvement on earlier ships. *[Zogolovitch Collection]*
Below: A circa 1910 Cunard Line advertisement showing the difference in fares between the three classes. *[Paul Louden-Brown Collection]*

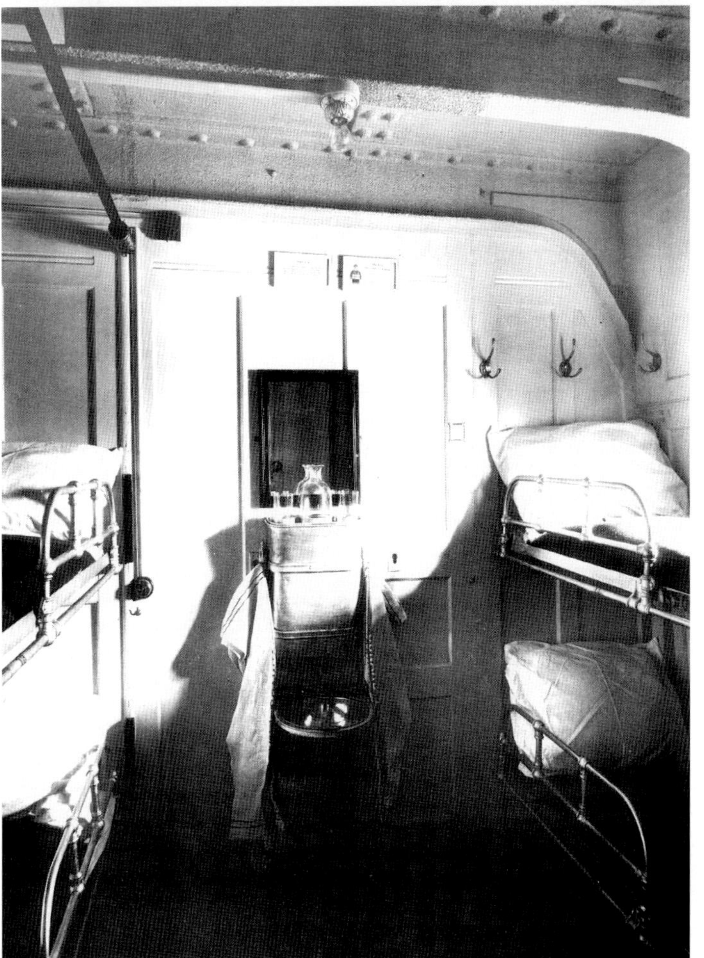

LUSITANIA and MAURETANIA. Largest Vessels in the world.

ULTONIA. CARPATHIA. PANNONIA. CAMPANIA.

FRANCONIA (Building). LACONIA (Building). IVERNIA. SAXONIA.

CUNARD LINE

INAUGURATED 1840

LARGEST, FINEST & FASTEST STEAMERS IN THE WORLD.

Sailings to NEW YORK and BOSTON on Tuesdays and Saturdays. (CALLING AT QUEENSTOWN.)

The CUNARD LINE have the largest, finest and fastest vessels afloat. They are of recent construction (being built under special supervision) and have all the modern improvements which can give strength and stability to the ship and comfort to the passengers.

All Passenger Steamers are fitted with Marconi's system of wireless telegraphy, and many are also fitted with the submarine signalling apparatus.

The Twin-Screw Ships "Ivernia," "Saxonia," "Caronia," and the Triple-Screw Turbine "Carmania," are among the finest steamers afloat, and their remarkable steadiness makes sea sickness practically impossible.

Third Class Families are berthed together. Single women are placed together in rooms by themselves; and Single men in rooms apart from all others. There is no separation on deck during the day.

Special Stewardesses are provided for Saloon, Second Cabin, and Third Class passengers, so that the requirements of the respective classes are well looked after.

Each Steamer carries an experienced Surgeon.

Rates of Passage from Liverpool or Queenstown.

	SALOON.	SECOND CABIN
MAURETANIA / LUSITANIA	£25 0s.	£12 10s.
CAMPANIA	£20 10s.	£10 10s.
CARONIA & CARMANIA	£19 10s.	£11 0s.
IVERNIA & SAXONIA	£16 10s.	£9 10s.

Second Cabin Rate from London, including third class rail ticket, 10/- extra.

Return Tickets issued on payment of the Combined Outward and Homeward Fares, without reduction.

The Saloon and Second Cabin Rates vary in accordance with the Steamer, season, position and number of Passengers in each room, all Passengers having equal privileges in the respective classes.

THIRD CLASS from — According to Steamer.
£6 15s. for U.S. CITIZENS, passengers to Canada, and Transit passengers.
£6 15s. plus 16s. Head Tax, for ALIENS settling in the United States.

Second Cabin and Third Class Passengers by New York steamers booked through to Boston or Philadelphia without extra charge.

Second Cabin and Third Class Passengers by Boston steamers booked through to New York or Philadelphia without extra charge.

Passengers booked through to all parts of the UNITED STATES and CANADA, CENTRAL AMERICA, and WEST COAST SOUTH AMERICA, also (via San Francisco and Vancouver) to CHINA, JAPAN, NEW ZEALAND and AUSTRALIA.

For further particulars apply to

PITT & SCOTT, 23, Cannon Street, LONDON. E.C

CARONIA. CARMANIA.

SOUTHERN RAILWAY

SALE BY AUCTION ON
THE "MAURETANIA"
of FURNISHINGS, PANELLING and APPOINTMENTS at SOUTHAMPTON DOCKS.

SECURE A SOUVENIR OF YOUR VOYAGE.

CHILDREN UNDER 14 YEARS OF AGE, HALF-FARE.

PRIVATE VIEW —May 9th.
GENERAL VIEW—May 10th, 11th and 13th.
SALE DAYS —May 14th to 17th inclusive, and 20th to 23rd inclusive.

Commencing 11.30 a.m. each day.

CHEAP RETURN TICKETS
from
LONDON
(Waterloo Station)

1st Class.	3rd Class.
s. d.	s. d.
20/-	13/3

Forward :	a.m.	a.m.	*Return :*	p.m.	p.m.
Waterloo ... ... dep.	8.30	9.30	Southampton West dep.	4.41	6.22
Southampton West arr.	10.29	11.31	Waterloo ... arr.	6.50	8.20

A special service of buses will run between Southampton West Station and the berth in Southampton Docks at which the "Mauretania" is accommodated, at a fare of 6d. each way.

Admission to Private View by Catalogue only, price 5/- each, and to General View and Sale Days, price 2/6d. each. One Catalogue will admit one person only.

Catalogues obtainable from Hampton & Sons, Auctioneers, 20, St. James's Square, London, S.W.1, at the Offices of Cunard White-Star, Ltd., Southampton, or at the Enquiry Office, Waterloo Station.

REFRESHMENTS will be obtainable on the "MAURETANIA."

TICKETS OBTAINABLE IN ADVANCE AT STATIONS AND AGENCIES.

Waterloo Station, S.E.1.

H. A. WALKER,
General Manager.

C.X. 1068/ 10/30435 April 23433

Printed by McCorquodale & Co. Ltd., London.

THE GREAT AUCTION OF 1935

On 2nd April 1935 Cunard White Star Line accepted a bid of £77,000 for *Mauretania* from J.W. Jobson, shipbroker for Britain's largest shipbreaker, Metal Industries Ltd. Robert McCrone (1893-1982) was the principal founder of this Glasgow-based breaker. His company came to fame when it bought many of the sunken German battleships raised by Ernest Cox at Scapa Flow. It also leased facilities at the Rosyth Naval Dockyard, Firth of Forth, Scotland for its demolition work. With the purchase of one of the most famous liners in the world, Robert McCrone and his partners decided to auction off the panelling, furniture, fixtures and fittings at Southampton and approached the well-known London auctioneers, Hampton and Sons, to arrange the sale. All removable Cunard White Star items such as linen, silver plate and glassware had been transferred to the company stores for use on other ships.

The auction was spread over eight days between 14th and 23rd May 1935 and consisted of 3,503 lots, some of which were required for her final voyage and could only be removed at the breaker's yard in Rosyth. A 191-page catalogue was produced which cost 2s.6d and allowed admittance to the viewing and sale. The public interest was phenomenal and the Southern Railway advertised cheap day return tickets from Waterloo Station, London. A special bus service also ran between Southampton station and *Mauretania*, whilst the Southern Railway Catering Department offered light refreshments in the Tourist Class Dining Saloon.

Day 1, Tuesday, 14th May 1935: First Class A Deck cabins, Library, Lounge, Smoke Room and Verandah Café

The auction began at 11.30am in the First Class Lounge. The attendees included former crew members who came to pay their last respects to the great liner. Among these was Robert Hubbard, the ship's Chief Electrical Engineer, who apart from three trips had been with the ship for her entire career. Hampton's auctioneer was John Fisk, who made his name in 1926 when he sold Sir Thomas Lawrence's famous painting 'Pinkie' for a world record £77,700. Before the start of the sale, Fisk mentioned what an honour it was for him to play a part in the final days of this wonderful and much-loved ship. It was also 'one of the rare occasions in which business and sentiment were joined and I hope that many will bid handsomely for a souvenir of this great ship.'

Lot 1 consisted of two small mahogany wardrobes with mirrored doors and drawers beneath, from a first class cabin on A Deck. After a slow start the hammer fell at £2-15-0 and the sale was underway. Bidding continued rather sluggishly despite exhortations from the auctioneer to 'think imperially' and to 'remember that this is the Jubilee year'. However, in the afternoon the First Class Library, Lounge and Smoke Room came up for sale and it was soon apparent that there were going to be three main bidders in this auction: Charles Boot, Harold Sandrey, and Walter Martin.

Charles Boot (1874-1945) bought most of the First Class Library except the dome and paid 120 guineas for the sycamore panelling, 64 guineas for four lots of doors, 13 guineas for the bookcases and 9 guineas for the 6 foot 8 inch-high arched mantle mirror. Boot was the head of the construction firm Henry Boot and Son, which had built more houses than any other in England. When asked what he intended to do with the library Boot, who had never sailed on *Mauretania*, replied that 'probably the big purchase will be utilised in some large public building, there to remain a permanent memorial to the proudest ship which has ever flown the British flag. The smaller oddments will be used in private dwellings.' In addition, he purchased a number of gilt bronze and cut crystal electric ceiling lights from the First Class Lounge as well as the various *fleur de pêche* lilac-coloured marble items including the sixteen pilasters and the fireplace.

The dome from the library was knocked down to Walter Martin (1867-1940) of Guernsey. He also bought the dome of the Lounge for 75 guineas and went on to buy the walnut panelling in the First Class Smoke Room for 270 guineas. He later acquired the magnificent 15th century Italian Renaissance-style chimney piece for 80 guineas. Equally vague about the reason for his purchases, he told a reporter that he planned to incorporate the panels in the Royal Hotel, Guernsey where it would be known as the Mauretania Smoke Room. He added 'I consider the stuff has been absolutely given away in relation to its quality for there is nothing to equal this panelling in the greatest hotels in the metropolis.' Martin was a larger than life character who once owned a leading London-based cigar and tobacco business, Martin Brothers.

Despite keen interest from Charles Boot, most of the mahogany First Class Lounge panelling was sold to Harold Sandrey (1872-1955) for 250 guineas. Sandrey, who was the Lloyd's agent on the Scilly Isles, said 'I have no special reason for buying the lounge panelling except that I have seen the 'Maury' go past my front door a good many times.' Relatively little is known about Harold Sandrey: he remained on the Scilly Isles until his death and was apparently a local 'entrepreneur'.

Towards the end of the first day's sale of 390 lots, the Secretary of the New Church in Kensington, London, A. Friend, bought the walnut panelling from the port and starboard vestibules which linked the First Class Smoke Room and the First Class Lounge.

Day 2, Wednesday, 15th May 1935: First Class B Deck port cabins, upper and lower Dining Saloon and hospital.

Whilst the second day's proceedings took place in the First Class Dining Saloon on C Deck, men were hard at work removing panelling sold the previous day from the first class public rooms and cabins. For the crew of the ship this was a very distressing sight. As the panels were removed, all the wiring was exposed as was the mass of hair and woollen packing which reduced movement and creaking of the wood. This also showed why fire was such a serious threat for these early liners and *Mauretania* was lucky not to have suffered more serious damage in the July 1921 fire, which broke out in a first class cabin and almost engulfed the First Class Dining Saloon. One of the most bizarre souvenirs recorded was when the First Class Lounge was being dismantled and the skeletons of two small rats found behind one of the panels. These former Tynesiders were claimed by a Southampton local and proudly taken ashore.

The largest lots on the second day were the fixtures and fittings of the First Class Dining Saloon. Walter Martin bought the upper section of the Dining Saloon including the weathered oak doors and panels, octagonal balustrade and the white enamelled and gilt dome. He paid in total 569 guineas for this section of the Dining Saloon and, with six days to go, it was soon apparent that he had a more elaborate plan for the fittings than he first envisaged and was talking about building a Hotel Mauretania. He was, however, less interested in the larger lower part of the Dining Saloon. Much of this was purchased by the London antique dealer Kerridges who hoped that it might be incorporated into a 'very interesting house'.

Although more private bidders attended the sale on Wednesday, progress was slow for cabin fixtures and fittings. Pairs of bedsteads fetched only £1 each, whilst the beautiful maple wood panelling in one of the first class cabins on B Deck sold for a mere 55 shillings. When proceedings finished at lot 783, the total raised so far was around £5,000.

Day 3, Thursday, 16th May 1935: First Class B Deck starboard and centre cabins

Each day the number attending the auction grew as people became more anxious to obtain a piece of the great ship, no matter how small. On the third day there were about a hundred more, mainly private buyers, than the previous day. The seven feet-high mahogany panels of the B Deck corridor were sold in lots, each ranging from 100 to 250 feet in length whilst wooden coat hangers with the ship's name were offered in bundles of a dozen and fetched about £1 per lot.

Day 4, Friday, 17th May 1935 First Class C Deck Barbers' Shops, Children's Room, Doctor's and Purser's cabins, starboard, port and centre cabins and Grand Staircase

On day four more buyers entered the fray. One of these was Ronald Avery (1899-1976), a great friend of Metal Industries' founder, Robert McCrone. He had also been the best man at his wedding. Avery was a well-known wine connoisseur who ran the family wine business, Avery's, in Park Street, Bristol. He planned a major refurbishment of the premises and came to the *Mauretania* sale hoping to purchase some panelling for his new venture. In the end he spent £1,850, an enormous sum in those days, on the star lot of the fourth day, the Grand Staircase. This consisted of all the fine figured walnut panelling and woodwork in the Italian Renaissance style spread over five decks and included the wrought iron dome on A Deck.

Whilst the Grand Staircase fetched such a high price, the white enamelled panelling in the First Class Children's Room, which included the five paintings by J.E. Mitchell illustrating the Nursery rhyme 'Four and twenty blackbirds', went for a song at just under ten pounds.

Day 5, Monday, 20th May 1935: First Class D Deck cabins, settees and chairs; Tourist A Deck Lounge and B Deck Drawing Room

After a weekend break the sale recommenced in the Dining Saloon on C Deck at 11.30am on Monday. Once again, there was great interest among the general public, especially in the 55 lots of first class chairs, bergéres, settees, lamps and mezzotint engravings. Pairs of chairs were knocked down for anything up to 13 guineas whilst half a dozen plated brass electric table lamps were sold for up to eight guineas a set.

The sale then moved to the Tourist Class Lounge where the 180 feet of teak panelling and glass dome were sold for 130 guineas. The final lots of the day were the seating and maple panelling from the Second Class Drawing Room. Whilst Walter Martin was out of the room having a whisky, Ronald Avery bought the panels for 36 guineas. Annoyed at having missed this lot, Martin bought the panels off Avery the following day for 60 guineas and Avery was overjoyed at such an easy profit. Martin had now acquired 440 lots and announced that he had rented space in one of the Southampton dock sheds to display his spoils. He also mentioned that he was thinking of building a Hotel Mauretania.

Day 6, Tuesday, 21st May 1935: Tourist B Deck Smoke Room, C Deck cabins, Dining Saloon, staircase and kitchens.

Walter Martin continued to dominate the proceedings, which took place in the Tourist Class Smoke Room on B Deck. He bought the mahogany panelling of that room for 110 guineas and the wrought iron framed glass dome for 42 guineas. However, Charles Boot and a Mr. Hanson purchased most of the American walnut panelling from the Tourist Class corridors of C Deck whilst the light oak panels and fixtures from the Tourist Class Dining Saloon were sold in six lots for a total of £182.14.0.

Although many of the public rooms and items from cabins found buyers, only 39 of the 75 lots from the galleys were sold. Among the culinary bargains were an electric rotary mixing machine with motor and switch board (£5); an 11-feet long deal flour trough with four hinged lids (£1); five large galvanised bins and twelve japanned canisters from the ship's Jewish Kitchen (ten shillings) and three large copper hot water urns with brass taps from the First Class Pantry on C Deck which went for fourteen shillings.

Day 7, Wednesday, 22nd May 1935: Tourist D Deck cabins; Third Class Upper Deck General and Smoke Rooms, D Deck cabins, chairs and carpets

The penultimate day of the sale was probably the least exciting of the entire auction and mainly consisted of tourist class cabin fittings, the Third Class General and Smoke Rooms and a miscellaneous series of lots of chairs, settees, rugs and carpets.

Day Eight, Thursday, 23rd May 1935: Third Class E Deck cabins, Dining Saloon, staircase, captain's, officers' and engineers' cabins, lifeboats, nautical instruments and letters from the ship's name

The final day attracted the largest attendance, especially as the lots on offer included bridge equipment, the captain's cabin and the brass names of the ship. Although Harold Sandrey's name cropped up regularly throughout the day, it was Walter Martin who was once again the dominant buyer.

The big event of the day was the sale of the captain's cabin and fittings. The auctioneer introduced these lots 3150 to 3173 by saying: 'I am sure you will realise that Sir Alfred Rostron was one of the finest commanders this country has known and I hope you will take something from his room to remember him by'. In fact, Captain Rostron did not attend the sale as he 'could not bear to watch the auctioneer hammering away my old ship piece by piece'. Twenty of the thirty lots in the captain's cabin were bought by Walter Martin, including panels, bunks and chest of drawers. The captains' chair and writing table sold for ten guineas a piece, whilst other souvenir hunters paid £2.10.0 for each of his cushions.

Although most of the machinery on the bridge was excluded from the sale, the flags and other items generated much interest, with Harold Sandrey buying most of the flags, including two Cunard house flags, for which he paid seven and a half guineas each. Sandrey also bought 14 of the lifeboats, the foremast crow's nest bell and two of the ship's magnetic compasses. A pair of binoculars engraved with *Mauretania*'s name fetched five guineas whilst Hanson paid £52.10.0 for the main triple bell whistle on the forward funnel. The organ pipe whistle on the second funnel went to an unknown buyer for £39.18.0. Lot 3414 was the 18 by 15 foot wood swimming pool fitted when *Mauretania* became a cruise ship. The letters of the *Mauretania* names on the port and starboard bow were sold to Martin for £150 a set. He then went on to pay 60 guineas for the *Mauretania* Liverpool stern lettering and also obtained a brass plate with the shipbuilder's name.

The final lots of the sale were a dozen teak batten and iron frame garden seats which fetched a total of £46.5.0. As the hammer came down for the last time for lot 3503, Walter Martin - who had bought more than a quarter of all the lots and had spent between £5,000 and £6,000 - rose from his seat and thanked Fisk for the courtesy he had displayed in conducting the auction. 'Three cheers for Mr. Fisk' and the attendees rose and gave three cheers followed by 'for he's a jolly good fellow'. The auction was concluded by the singing of the National Anthem. An exhausted Fisk said afterwards that the sale had exceeded his expectations and that 'it is the biggest auction in my career from the point of view of the number of lots offered and I am tonight a very satisfied and contented man.' For *Mauretania*'s new owner, Metal Industries, the sale had also been far better than expected and achieved a grand total of £14,877.

In the seven months prior to the Hampton's auction, *Mauretania* remained at Berth 108 in Southampton's Western Docks. In April 1935, she was joined by White Star Line's *Olympic*, which was sold for demolition in September. *[Michael Pocock Collection]*

By direction of Metal Industries Limited, Glasgow

ADMIT ONE to Public View, Friday, Saturday and Monday,
May 10th, 11th and 13th, 1935, and Sale Days.

The Appointments, Equipment and Panelling of

The Mauretania

HAMPTON & SONS,

Auctioneers,

20, St. James's Square,
London, S.W.1

By direction of Metal Industries Limited, Glasgow.

SOUTHAMPTON.

CATALOGUE OF THE

COSTLY APPOINTMENTS FURNISHINGS and PANELLING

OF

THE

Mauretania

Including Settees and Easy Chairs in Moquette and Tapestry, Sets of Chairs in the Chippendale and Hepplewhite taste, Dining and Occasional Tables, Bookcases, Cabinets, Fine Quality Wilton and Axminster Carpets.

MAGNIFICENT PANELLING

of Weathered Oak, Harewood, Mahogany, Walnut, &c., in the Francois 1er, Italian Renaissance and 18th Century English Styles.

Costly Appointments of the Numerous Cabins

in Mahogany, Walnut, Satinwood, Maple and Birch, Marble and Wood Mantelpieces and Columns, Sanitary Goods, Equipment of Ship's Cuisine, Fire Appliances, Ornamental Electric Light Fittings, Fans, Navigating Instruments, Electric Cranes and

THE LIFE BOATS

HAMPTON & SONS

Are instructed to Sell the above by Auction

ABOARD THE VESSEL, IN SOUTHAMPTON DOCKS

(By permission of the Southern Railway Company),

On TUESDAY, MAY 14th, 1935,

And 7 FOLLOWING DAYS, at 11.30 o'clock each day.

Private View (admission by Catalogue only, price 5/- each), Thursday, May 9th; General View (admission by Catalogue only, price 2/6 each), Friday, Saturday and Monday, May 10th, 11th and 13th, from 9.30 a.m. to 4.30 p.m. each day.

Catalogues from the Auctioneers, at their Offices:—

Branch Offices:
Wimbledon & Hampstead.

20, St. James's Square,
London, S.W. 1.

Telegrams: "Selanlet, Piccy, London." Telephone: Whitehall 6767 (9 lines).

Or from CUNARD WHITE STAR LIMITED, SOUTHAMPTON.

The auction underway in the First Class Lounge.
[A. Andrews Collection]

The MAURETANIA, Southampton Docks

Each Purchaser will be required by Messrs. HAMPTON & SONS to fill in this slip and hand same to the Auctioneers' Clerk on making the first purchase.

Purchaser's Name ....

Address in full ....

....

Telephone :

Before the auction, a series of photographs were taken of Metal Industries staff holding the auction catalogue and examining various lots. Wearing a black hat is Max Wilkinson, later Managing Director of Metal Industries subsidiary, Shipbreaking Industries Ltd. Top left: The First Class Lounge. Top right: Opposite the bow windows of the First Class Lounge on the Boat Deck. Bottom: On the bridge. *[University of Newcastle upon Tyne Collection]*

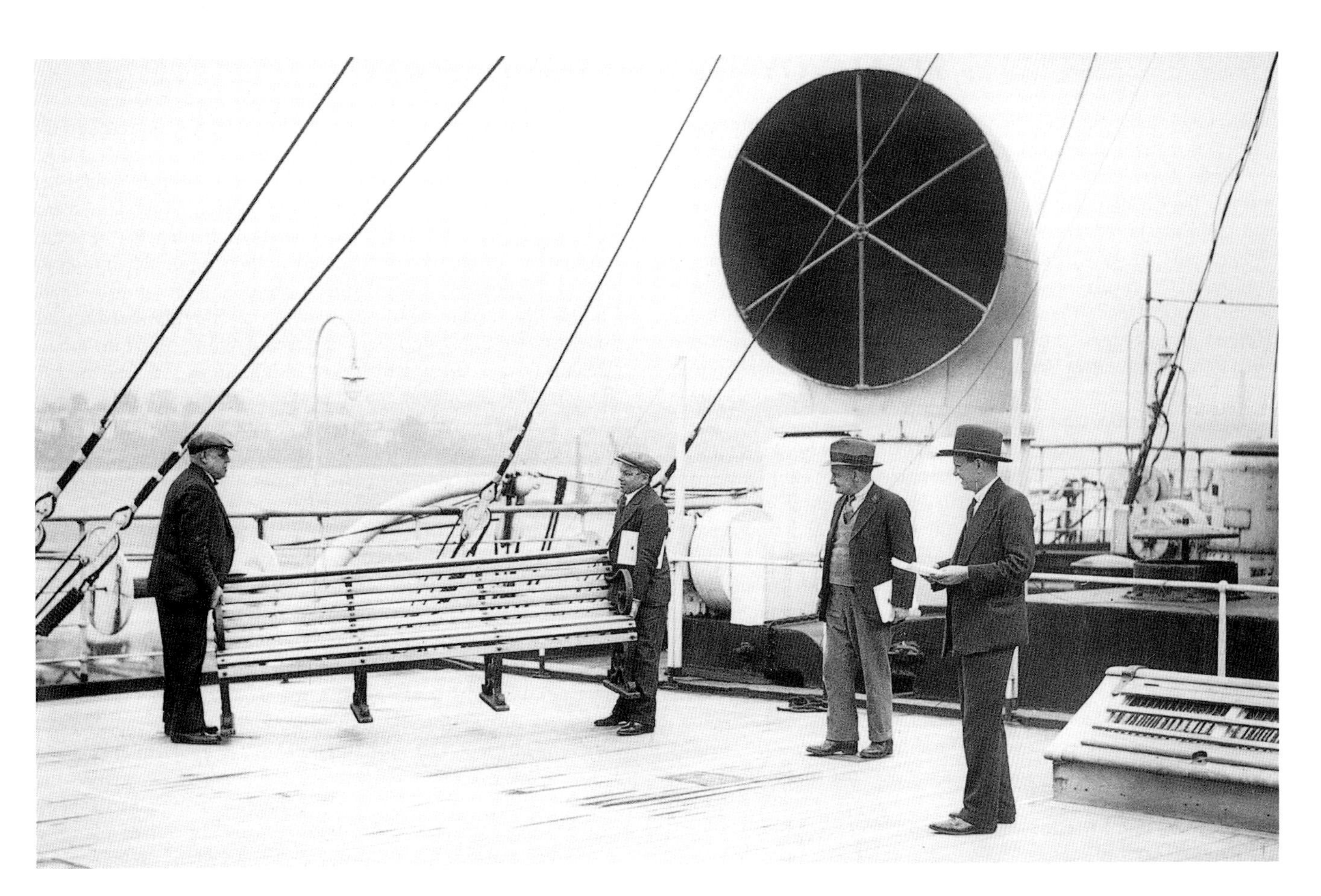

One of twelve teak batten and iron frame benches, which were the last lots in the sale. This photo was taken in the small deck space between the first and second funnel, which was used for deck games and boxing matches. *[University of Newcastle upon Tyne Collection]*

As the sale progressed, carpenters from Hamptons removed fixtures and panelling. This is the First Class Smoke Room. Compare this view with the one on page 53. *[Southern Daily Echo]*

FINAL VOYAGE AND DEMOLITION

Mauretania remained at her berth for another five weeks after the auction as material was removed from the ship and she was prepared for her final voyage to Scotland. With her white hull rust-streaked, most of the lifeboats missing, her whistles removed, and her fore and main masts reduced so that she could pass under the Forth Bridge, she looked in a sorry state. As a local newspaper commented: 'rarely has a more pathetic sight been seen at Southampton Docks than the passing of the old Cunarder, the *Mauretania* last night.' Incidentally, since 12th April 1935, she had been joined in lay-up at Berth 108 by another famous transatlantic liner, White Star Line's *Olympic*, which had also once been the world's largest ship.

On Sunday the 1st of July, her final day in Southampton, an informal dinner was held aboard *Mauretania.* The Southern Railway, which ran the docks, issued special passes for those wishing to see the old veteran for the last time, and from 6pm admission was free. Thousands crammed the quayside as she prepared to sail at 9pm. Aboard was a skeleton crew commanded by Captain A. T. Brown. She also carried 85 passengers, including Walter Martin and many dignitaries. Despite not wishing to board his old ship, Captain Sir Arthur Rostrum was there to watch *Mauretania* as she moved slowly away from Berth 108. On her foremast she flew a 20-foot long pennant with the figures 1907 to 1929, a reminder of her 22-years of transatlantic records. There were no streamers, just the sound of the 'Last Post' and the strains of 'Auld Lang Syne' played by the Docks and Marine Band. Her old rival *Olympic*, also destined for the scrap yard later that year, added to the sombre occasion with a mournful blast from her whistles and a pall of black smoke from her funnels. Dropping her pilot at the Nab, *Mauretania* sailed out of Southampton Water accompanied by a myriad of small boats.

For those on board, *Mauretania* must have been a very eerie ship as she sailed up the East Coast at a fraction of her normal speed and with most of her interiors stripped bare. By late Monday she passed Scarborough and the following morning stopped two miles off the mouth of the River Tyne for an hour to say farewell to those who built her 28 years earlier. Thousands came down to see her and in return, rockets were fired from her bridge. The Lord Mayor of Newcastle, Councillor and shipowner R.S. Dalgleish, also received the following radio message: 'Thank you for your greeting. For 28 years I have striven to be a credit to you, and now my day is done. Though I pass on, may Tyneside ever reach out to further and greater triumphs. With pride and affection I greet you. Farewell - *Mauretania*.' A flotilla of boats, including the tug *Plover* with the Lord Mayor aboard, went out to see the ship. Several of the town's notables went aboard for a short visit and met with Captain Brown on the bridge. Once they had disembarked she continued her slow journey northwards. Later that day she passed Amble, the last port in England, and was sent a message by Mr. Goodges, Clerk to Amble Urban District Council: 'Amble to *Mauretania*. Greetings from Amble, last port in England, to still the greatest ship on the seas.' In response, he received: '*Mauretania* to Urban Council, Amble, to the last and kindliest port in England, greetings and thanks. *Mauretania*.'

The 1907 to 1929 pennant being lowered at Rosyth. *[Ken Saunders Collection]*

At 6am on Wednesday, 4th July *Mauretania* reached the Firth of Forth. Assisted by the Leith Salvage and Towage Co. Ltd. tugs *Herwit* (254/1904) and *Oxcar* (252/1919) and still under her own steam, she passed beneath the Forth Bridge. Rust stained and with black smoke billowing from her two aft funnels, the scene inspired one of the most evocative paintings of an old ship on its way to the breakers since Turner's *Fighting Téméraire* in 1838. Charles Pears' painting of *Mauretania* was commissioned for the Tourist Class Smoking Room on Cunard White Star Line's new flagship *Queen Mary*, which was fitting out at the John Brown Shipyard, Clydebank, on the other side of Scotland.

As she was warped into the entrance lock of the Rosyth Dockyard, a lone piper in the full dress of the Royal Stuart Clan played the lament 'Flowers of the Forest'. Once in the main basin, *Mauretania* turned into the No. 1 Dry Dock, which was to be her final resting place.

Not surprisingly, there was considerable interest in her arrival and Metal Industries decided to allow visitors into the dockyard on the following Sunday, 8th July. For a shilling a head it was possible to visit not only *Mauretania* but also the upturned 1916-built German battleship *Bayern*, which was being demolished in the adjoining dry dock. 8th July was a hot summer's day and an estimated 100,000 people turned up, with the 500-capacity car park fully utilised. The queue for the ship was over a mile long and at times was six or seven persons deep. Many abandoned the queue, which at its peak involved a wait of up to two hours, whilst 20,000 paid a shilling a head to have a final look around *Mauretania*. £400 of the proceeds was given to charity.

Demolition commenced on 21st August. By February the following year, she had been cut down to the lower deck aft and the upper deck amidships. In August work was completed on the tidal beach at No. 3 Yard. Metal Industries almost certainly made a profit from its purchase as she yielded 22,525 tons of ferrous (iron) scrap, 1,255 tons of non-ferrous (metals or alloys that are free of iron) material and 1,350 tons of sundries, mainly timber. Much of the teak decking was sold to the Hughes Bolckow Shipbreaking Co. Ltd. at Blyth, Northumberland, which specialised in producing teak chairs, benches and other garden furniture.

However, that was not the end of the *Mauretania* name. In late 1936 Cunard White Star Line placed an order with the Birkenhead shipyard Cammell, Laird and Co. Ltd. for a similar sized ship, which was designed for the London-New York route. As the British Board of Trade did not usually allow two ships of the same name on the British register of shipping, Cunard White Star wished to safeguard the use of the name until its new *Mauretania* was launched on 28th July 1938. It persuaded the Southampton, Isle of Wight and South of England Royal Mail Steam Packet Co. Ltd. (Red Funnel) to change the name of one of its elderly paddle steamers *Queen* (345/1902) to *Mauretania* for two years between 1936 and 1938. Although she lasted almost as long as her namesake, the second *Mauretania*, intended for an intermediate service, and the ability to replace *Queen Elizabeth* or *Queen Mary* when they were out of service, sailed into a fast changing world of transatlantic travel. She never achieved the fame of the '*Old Ship*' and was sold for scrap in 1965.

Two aerial views of *Mauretania* shortly before she sailed on her final voyage. Rust-streaked, her whistles and most of the lifeboats had been removed. Her fore and main masts were also reduced so that she could pass under the Forth Bridge. *[Top: Luis Miguel Correia Collection; Bottom: University of Newcastle upon Tyne Collection]*

A view of her stern not long before her departure. *[University of Newcastle upon Tyne Collection]*

Above left: 'Chief mourners' boarding the ship. *[Zogolovitch Collection]*
Above right: Captain Brown saying farewell to the Mayor of Southampton, Councillor G. Waller. *[Southern Daily Echo]*

Watched by a huge crowd, *Mauretania* left Southampton at 9pm on Sunday 1st of July, 1935. Note the newsreel camera and band. *[Maurizio Elizeo Collection]*

On Tuesday morning she reached the Tyne flying a 20ft-long pennant on her foremast with the dates 1907 to 1929. *[George Scott Collection]*

Early the following day, *Mauretania* passed under the Forth Bridge. *[George Scott Collection]*

Assisted by tugs *Herwit* and *Oxcar*, she entered the Rosyth Naval Dockyard. *[University of Newcastle upon Tyne Collection]*

A lone piper played the lament 'Flowers of the Forest'.
[University of Newcastle upon Tyne Collection]

Finished with engines. Captain Brown (right) and possibly the Chief Engineer. *[Zogolovitch Collection]*

A view from the 100-ton crane at No 1 Dry Dock. The crane can be seen in the photograph below. In the adjoining dry dock was the upturned 1916-built German battleship *Bayern*, which had been scuttled at Scapa Flow in 1919. *[University of Newcastle upon Tyne Collection]*

Another dramatic scene from the 100-ton crane in September 1935, with only her forward funnel remaining upright.
[University of Newcastle upon Tyne Collection]

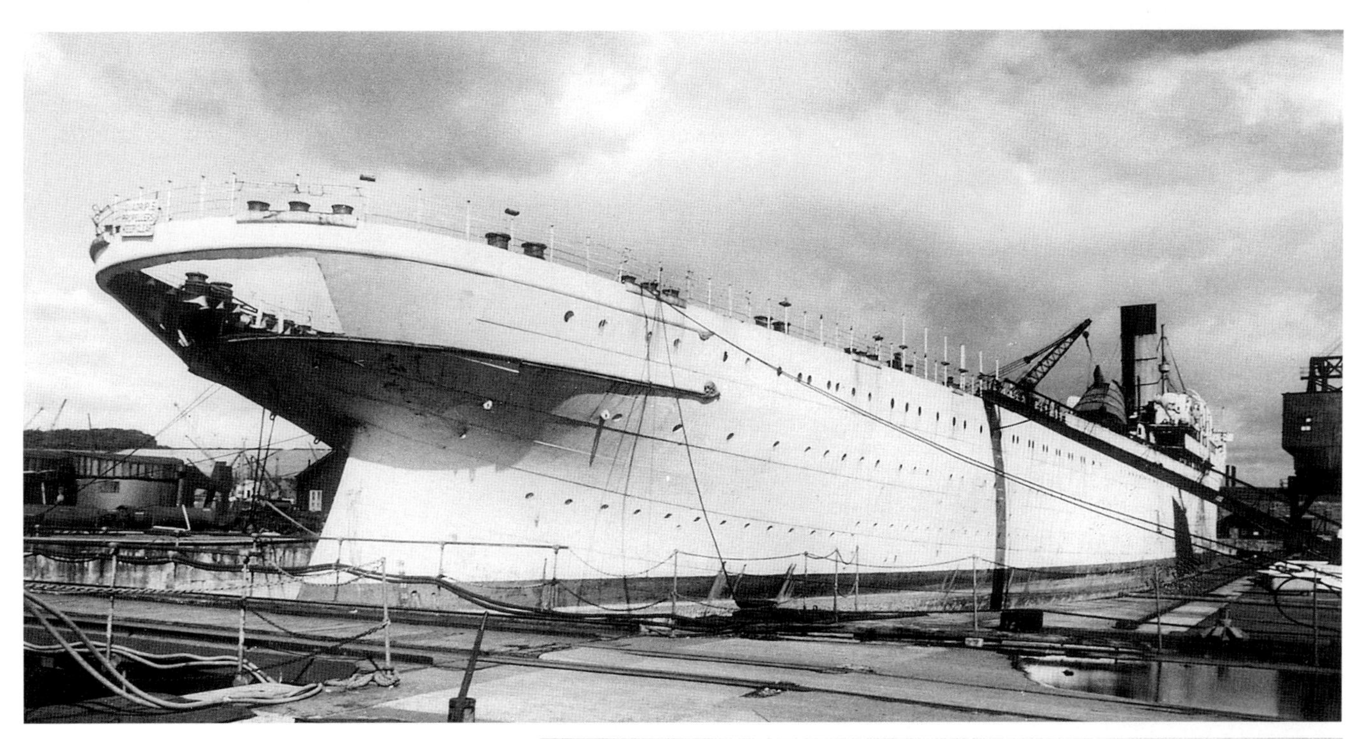

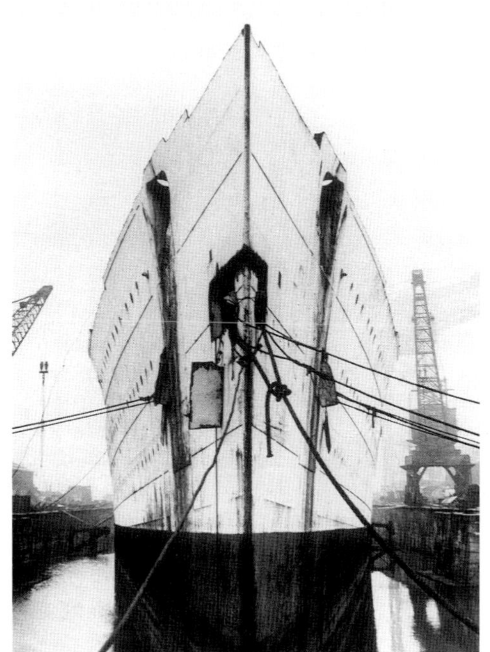

Because of her high air draught and the strong cross winds in the Firth of Forth, *Mauretania* was kept afloat during demolition. The hull had to be carefully cut down and firmly moored to avoid any shifting in her balance. These photographs were taken during the latter part of 1935. *[University of Newcastle upon Tyne Collection]*

Left: Workmen removing her port side letters. *[University of Newcastle upon Tyne Collection]*

Middle: Once the hull was cut down to the waterline, it was towed to the tidal beach at No 3 Yard, where her remains were demolished sometime in the second half of 1936. *[Maurizio Elizeo Coll-ection]*

Bottom right: Whilst a new *Mauretania* was under construction, the name was borne from 1936 to 1938 by the Southampton-based Red Funnel Line paddle steamer *Queen*. Here she is as *Mauretania* on an excursion from Bournemouth Pier in July 1937 *[Ken Saunders Collection]* and (left) passing Old Harry Rocks. Dorset. *[Peter Newall Collection]*

PART TWO

RESURRECTION

THE MAURETANIA SYNDICATE

To promote his grandiose plan for a Hotel Mauretania, Walter Martin decided to re-erect *Mauretania*'s main public rooms in Southampton Docks. He approached the Southern Railway Company during the May auction and rented space in Cargo Sheds 14-16, on the southside of the old Inner Dock.

Together with a group of investors, Martin also formed, probably in August 1935, a Guernsey-based company called The Mauretania Syndicate Ltd. Among the items owned by the company were many of the purchases made by Harold Sandrey, including the First Class Lounge. However, it is not clear if Mr. Sandrey was a member of the group or if he sold his pieces to The Mauretania Syndicate.

At great expense the rooms were reassembled at Southampton using skilled carpenters and architectural plasterers. These included the upper level of the First Class Dining Saloon, complete with its ornate white and gilt plaster dome, the First Class Smoke Room without the glass roof, and the First Class Lounge minus its dome. The complete Tourist Class Lounge and Smoke Room were also on display as was the Captain's Cabin, a number of Regal Suites, mahogany First Class corridor panelling and a number of sundry items including the port and stern lettering, foremast crow's nest bell, shipbuilder's plate, compasses and a flag staff with the Cunard Line house flag.

A limited edition, leather-bound prospectus was issued which showed the various rooms and cabins erected for view. The items were offered for sale as one lot. The 52 page book also incorporated a pull-out plan by the well-known architects Sir John Burnet, Tait and Lorne showing a suggested lay-out of the rooms for the ground floor of a restaurant, club or hotel.

On 30th October 1935 the New York Herald Tribune carried a story headed: 'Ghost of Junked Mauretania to Walk as British Hotel Here'. It incorrectly stated that a London syndicate had plans to build a Hotel Mauretania in New York. Martin's idea was, of course, to interest an American syndicate in purchasing the Mauretania public rooms and re-erect them somewhere in the United States,

There was little interest in the idea and the Syndicate became desperate to offload the *Mauretania* fittings. On 14th January 1936 J. Wild, the Syndicate's Secretary, wrote to the Purser of the Cunard White Star liner *Majestic* enclosing a prospectus and suggested that he showed it to passengers who might be interested in seeing the rooms in Southampton docks. He added: 'They might be prospective buyers, or simply interested to renew association, and I would be pleased to show them over on presentation of your card with the visitor's name written on it. And I would add that, in the event of a sale being made through your direct introduction, we should be pleased to arrange for you to receive a generous appreciation in tangible form. The amount would naturally depend on the nature of the transaction.'

In the second half of 1936, The Mauretania Syndicate Ltd. went into receivership. Charles Boot bought the doors from the First Class Smoke Room and Dining Saloon from the liquidators and these were incorporated into his new film studio complex at Pinewood. The disposal of the remaining items from The Mauretania Syndicate took place in an auction held in Cargo Shed 16, Southampton Docks on the 21st and 22nd October 1936. Acting on behalf of the Receiver, the auction was run by a local auctioneer, William Burrough Hill. Among the sale items were a number of the public rooms, cabins, three Aubusson tapestries from the First Class Lounge and the brass port and stern letters for which Walter Martin originally paid £213.

On the first day of the sale, the 280 lots only fetched about £160. The sale did not fare much better the following day, with no interest in the panelling for the First Class Lounge, First Class Smoke Room and Second Class Drawing Room. These were later sold privately for only £150. The ship's letters went to a Plymouth buyer for a mere £11 whilst the three magnetic compasses fetched only £1.12.6d. The Aubusson tapestries also attracted no bids and a group of flags only managed 22s. All this was far short of the £5,000 - £6,000 spent by Martin at the May 1935 sale, a sum which did not include the immense cost of reconstructing the rooms nor the rental of the sheds.

Around this time another key player in the post-*Mauretania* story entered the frame, Frederick. H. Bartlett, a Leatherhead-based speculative builder. Apparently he was a South African with a goatee beard who had a striking resemblance to the then Prime Minister of South Africa, Jan Smuts. In 1918 he took over a long-established Leatherhead building firm W. H. Brown Ltd. He constructed numerous buildings in the south Leatherhead area but during the Great Depression the company got into financial difficulties and was forced to close in 1933. Despite this setback, Bartlett restarted his business soon afterwards as F. H. Bartlett of Givons Grove, Leatherhead. His letterhead described himself as an Estate Developer who specialised in the 'Reconstruction of Old-World Houses'.

Frederick Bartlett became involved with *Mauretania* after the failure of The Mauretania Syndicate. Whether he started off as an agent for the Receiver is uncertain. He did, however, acquire some of the material, and was involved in the sale of a major part of the First Class Lounge to Ronald Avery in Bristol. He also sold the Tourist Class Drawing Room and Captain's Cabin to a wealthy property developer, Thomas Cullen, who lived nearby in Tyrrell's Wood, Leatherhead. These were incorporated into Mr. Cullen's new house at Hamworthy, Poole which was designed and built by Frederick Bartlett.

The mahogany panelled Tourist Class Smoke Room was brought to Givons Grove and was partially reassembled near the Bartlett workshops. The entire room was on sale for £250, 'free on lorry at Leatherhead'. What happened to this room and its dome is unclear, as is the whereabouts of much of the First Class Dining Saloon. However, other items from the doomed The Mauretania Syndicate such as the ship's letters have resurfaced and are mentioned later in the book.

The PUBLIC ROOMS, Regal Suites and Mementoes of R.M.S. "MAURETANIA."

OFFERED FOR SALE

The 1st Class SMOKE ROOM, size 50 feet × 50 feet, in quartered French Walnut ... ... Pages 18 to 23
The 1st Class LOUNGE, size 55 feet × 65 feet, in African Mahogany ... ... Pages 24 to 29
The 1st Class DINING SALOON, size 64 feet × 68 feet, in Weathered Oak (Dancing Enclosure 26 feet diameter)... ... Pages 30 to 35
The DRAWING ROOM, size 41 feet × 30 feet, in figured Maplewood ... ... Pages 36 to 39
The TOURIST LOUNGE and SMOKE ROOM, size 38 feet × 52 feet, in inlaid Mahogany ... Pages 40 to 43
31 REGAL SUITES— a few are shown on Pages 44 to 50

1 in inlaid Sycamore.	1 in inlaid Birch.
2 in inlaid Harewood.	1 in stained Birch.
1 in figured Satin Birch.	2 in inlaid Mahogany.
5 in inlaid Satin Birch.	1 in panelled Mahogany.
3 in inlaid Satin Wood.	10 in carved white enamel Adams style.
4 in inlaid Maplewood.	

SUNDRIES ... ... Pages 51 and 52

Ship's Bell.	Binnacles.
Ship's Name, in 24 and 18 inch brass letters.	Flagstaff.
	Shipbuilders' Plate.

The Photographs on the following pages are peeps only into the Heart of the Grand Old Lady.

The Rooms are shown :

(a) **As they were on the ship ;**

(b) **In the course of re-erection ; and**

(c) **The rooms completely rebuilt inside the Dock Sheds at Southampton.**

A suggested PLAN.

At the end of the book, is a lay-out of the rooms for the ground floor of an Hotel, a Restaurant or a Club, suggested and drawn by the eminent architects Sir John Burnet, Tait and Lorne.

NOTE.

The temporarily rebuilt rooms of the "MAURETANIA" are in Sheds 14/16, Old Docks, Southampton, and may be viewed at any time by appointment.

The "MAURETANIA" Syndicate Ltd.,
Guernsey, Channel Islands.

Cable Addresses :
Mauretania, Guernsey.
Mauretania, Southampton.

[Zogolovitch Collection]

In Cargo Sheds 14-16, old inner Southampton Docks, skilled carpenters and plasterers painstakingly reconstructed a number of the *Mauretania*'s public rooms. Top left: the First Class Lounge being reassembled. Top right: the rebuilt First Class Smoke Room, including the well-known octagonal table. Left: plasterers starting to erect a section of the First Class Dining Saloon dome. Bottom left: sections of the dome before re-erection. Bottom right: The Upper Dining Saloon and the white and gilt plaster dome re-erected in the shed. *[Zogolovitch Collection]*

Top: Workmen putting the finishing touches to the maple-panelled Second Class Drawing Room. Middle and bottom: The Second Class Smoke Room with its wrought iron dome and mahogany panelling was also completely rebuilt in the dock shed. This dome was later reassembled in Frederick Bartlett's workshop at Leatherhead. *[Zogolovitch Collection]*

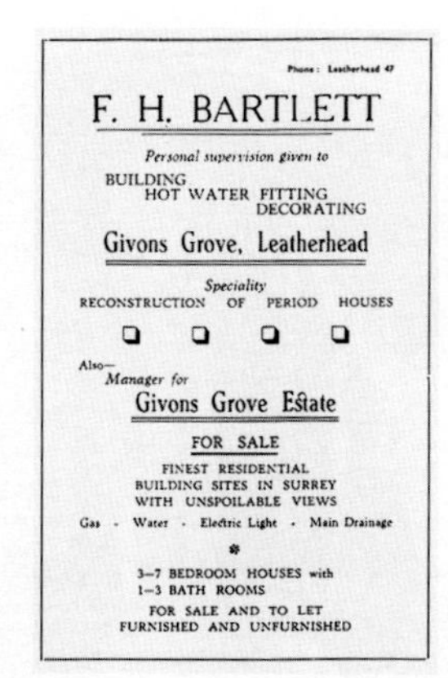

Above: A 1935 advertisement for Frederick Bartlett's new company.
Below: Liquidator's sale announcement, complete with typographic errors.
[Southampton Daily Echo]

ON WEDNESDAY AND THURSDAY NEXT

By direction of the Receiver and Manager of the "Mauretania" Syndicate, Ltd.

SOUTHAMPTON DOCKS.

Important SALE by AUCTION of the remainder of the costly PANELLING, FURNISHINGS AND APPOINTMENTS OF THE "MAURETANIA,"

including a number of Public Rooms and Cabins (several as re-erected, others as dismantled), a large number of Mahogany and other Doors, Double and Single Mahogany Compactums, 2 complete sets of Brass Letters "Mauretania," the Genealogical Tree of the Pilgrim Fathers, three "Aubusson" Tapestries, 28 feet Lifeboat for 57 persons, with gear, Kelvin's Magnetic Compasses, and numerous other items, which

WM. BURROUGH HILL

is instructed to SELL by AUCTION, in Shed No. 16, Southampton Docks (by permission of the Southern Railway Company), on WEDNESDAY and THURSDAY, 21st and 22nd October shrdlu hrdl rdll 21st and 22nd October, 1936, commencing at 12 noon each day. Admission to Docks (No. 5 Gate) by catalogue only (price 1/- each), to be obtained at the Dock Gate No. 5, or from the Auctioneer, 7, Hanover Buildings, Southampton.

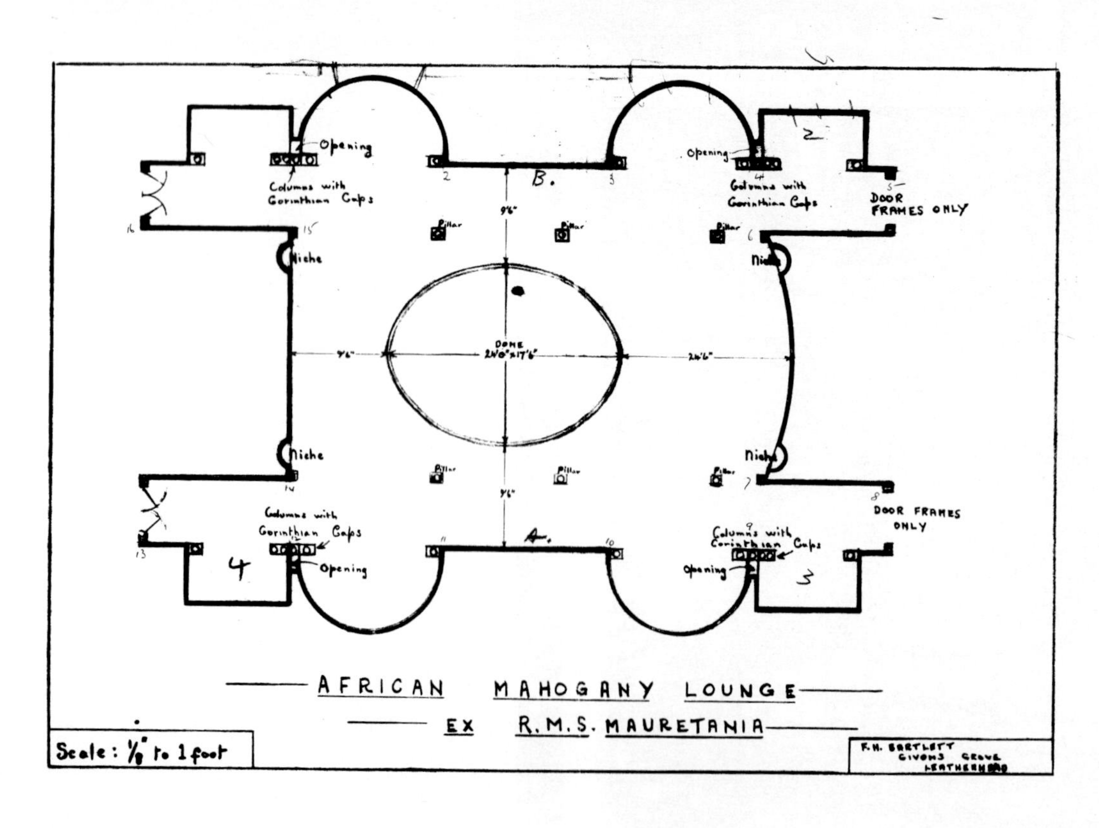

Top left: In this 1920s photo of the W. H. Brown workforce, Frederick Bartlett is the bald man with a beard in the centre of the fifth row back. *[Leatherhead Museum Collection]*
Left: Frederick Bartlett produced this plan of the First Class Lounge for Ronald Avery in Bristol. *John Avery Collection]*

WALTER MARTIN AND THE ROYAL HOTEL, GUERNSEY

On the 29th July 1940, the day after Walter Martin died at his home on Guernsey, the 'Guernsey Evening Post' devoted a full page to this colourful character who made and lost three fortunes during his lifetime.

A native of Guernsey, Martin was born in 1867, the son of a former Guernsey harbourmaster. He and his brother Arthur started a small clothing shop in Mill Street, St. Peter Port before moving to Maddox Street where they had a clothing and tobacconist firm. The brothers' next shop was in the High Street where it became one of Guernsey's best-known businesses. In the early part of the 20th century, the Martins also developed a successful cigar and tobacco business in London. Martin Brothers became one of London's leading cigar shippers and tobacco manufacturers. During the First World War, Walter Martin formed the Overseas Club, which raised money for tobacco and cigarettes to be sent to the forces fighting abroad. An estimated one million pounds was raised and the immense task of manufacturing and packing the tobacco and cigarettes took place in Guernsey, overseen by Martin.

Walter Martin (1867-1940) *[Guernsey Evening Post]*

Much of Walter Martin's personal life is a mystery. In 1938 he arranged a special showing at the St. Peter Port Gaumont cinema of Frank Capra's film 'You can't take it with you'. Before the film started, he gave a speech about his own experience with money. In 1918, he had suffered his first bankruptcy and around this time Martin Brothers became Martins Ltd. The company was acquired by Rothmans in 1937 and remained part of this company until its merger with British American Tobacco in 1999.

Walter Martin was certainly a great gambler and claimed that in 1920 he was 'the man who broke the bank at Monte Carlo.' The famous film with the same name was not, however, about him. On a single day the impoverished Martin broke the bank three times and left the casino half a million francs richer. In the 1920s he returned to Guernsey and in 1930 bought Guernsey's leading hotel, the Royal Hotel. At that time, it had 120 bedrooms, 35 bathrooms and a staff of 60.

The Royal Hotel was one of the most significant buildings on the sea front of St. Peter Port. It started life in the 18th century as the town house of a Guernsey Lieutenant-Bailiff. In 1843, it became Lewis's Marine Hotel and with a change of ownership, its name was changed to Gardner's Royal Hotel in 1871. The hotel expanded in the late 19th century when properties either side were incorporated into the site and it became one of Guernsey's premier hotels. Walter Martin's ownership of the Royal Hotel lasted just over a year until financial problems forced him to sell it to the Commercial Company of the Channel Islands, a subsidiary of the well-known Guernsey wine and tobacco company, Bucktrout and Company. Martin, however, retained a sizeable shareholding in the hotel and remained managing director for the rest of his life. Although he was a great catalyst in promoting Guernsey as a tourist destination, he came up with a number of grandiose schemes in the 1930s which never quite got off the ground. One of these was to redevelop the site of the Royal Hotel and build a grand hotel. He did, however, modernise the hotel and introduced a distinctive orange and marigold colour scheme for the hotel staff uniforms which was also used for cars and boats associated with the hotel.

Despite the failure of The Mauretania Syndicate and the idea of building a Mauretania Hotel in New York, Walter Martin brought some of the fixtures and fittings to Guernsey where they were incorporated into the Royal Hotel. Most of the pieces in the Royal Hotel from *Mauretania* appear to have been tables, chairs and mahogany wardrobes. In 1965 a major refurbishment saw many of the *Mauretania* items either sold or broken up for firewood. Two *Mauretania* rooms, 202 and 208, survived until the 28th June 1992 when a fire broke out on the top floor and they were ruined by water pumped into the building. In 1999 the hotel was demolished and new buildings have been built on what is one of Guernsey's most valuable pieces of real estate.

Walter Martin's final years were spent at his house 'The Crabpot', L'Islet on the northern coast of Guernsey. Some of the Mauretania panelling is believed to have been installed in his study but, during the German Occupation of Guernsey, the house was taken over by the Germans and stripped of its fittings and the wood burned for fuel. Although the house on the site is named 'La Bonade' (Guernsey French for crabpot), nothing remains of the original Martin house. In fact, during two visits to Guernsey not a single *Mauretania* item was found and there is also little evidence of the larger than life man whose original *Mauretania* purchases of 1935 are scattered about mainland Britain.

THE BOAT HOUSE, POOLE

Almost entirely landlocked, Poole Harbour in Dorset is the world's second largest natural harbour and one of the most beautiful places in England. With its numerous islands and inlets, it covers 28 square miles of water with 96 miles of mostly muddy and sandy shoreline. It is a yachtsman's paradise and at one time boasted five yacht clubs, including The Royal Motor Yacht Club founded in 1905, as the marine arm of the Royal Automobile Club.

In the 1930s, apart from the ancient trading town of Poole, much of the area around Poole Harbour had not been built on. The harbour entrance at Sandbanks was covered in sand dunes with only a few houses. Nowadays, Sandbanks property prices are amongst the highest in the world. To the south west of the town of Poole is Hamworthy, established as a port in Roman times, and now the departure point for ferries and high speed catamarans to France and the Channel Islands. From here the coastline meanders northward to Rockley Point and the estate owned by Lord Rockley. Although much of Hamworthy is now covered in houses, when the London property developer Thomas Cullen bought a plot of land in the early 1930s on what was called the Lake Estate, the whole area was just sand dunes and heathland. To the east of the plot was a shipyard which built ferro-concrete barges during the First World War whilst on the other side was an old wooden pier once used by barges carrying clay from the now-disused Doultons' clay workings. Poole is, of course, famous for Poole Pottery and the old claypits formed a large lake, hence the name Lake Estate.

Thomas (Tom) J. Cullen (1885-1965) was chairman and managing director of London County Freehold and Leasehold Properties Ltd., also known as Key Flats, one of the largest property companies in London. A keen yachtsman, Cullen owned an eight-metre yacht *Emily II*, which was built at Teignmouth in 1929. Although he had a house on an estate called Tyrrell's Wood, near Leatherhead in Surrey, the plot off Lake Drive in Hamworthy was bought as a retreat for himself and his sailing friends. He employed the Leatherhead-based speculative builder Frederick. H. Bartlett to design a house and boat shed on his new plot of land.

The plans for the new Cullen residence in Hamworthy were most unusual. Designed in a Mediterranean-style, the two-story house has a distinctive blue pantile roof. It also has a roof terrace with wonderful views to the south and west of Poole Harbour.

Situated at the end of a cul-de-sac, the property is approached up a curved concrete driveway. At the front of the brick-built house a terraced garden leads down to a sandy beach and a large 30 by 13-foot wooden boat shed, which also has a blue pantile roof. This had an upper floor with bunks and mattresses for extra sleeping accommodation. A private slipway for the boats also led up to the boat shed.

The interior of the main house was a complete contrast to the modern-style exterior. In October 1936 Bartlett acquired from the liquidators of the failed Mauretania Syndicate a number of officer's cabins, including the Captain's Cabin, and the maple panelling from the Second Class Drawing Room. The main entrance of what became known as the Boat House is on the upper floor with its balustraded oval-shaped gallery looking down onto the lounge-dining room. The gallery also incorporates four *Mauretania* hollow Corinthian columns and a glass skylight, which came from another liner. Overlooking the water are three ship's officer's cabins, with bunks. In one of these bedrooms is the dressing chest-of-drawers and mirror from the captain's bedroom. In one corner of the gallery landing are wardrobes which came from White Star Line's *Majestic* ex *Bismarck*. Sold in 1936, she was converted into a Royal Navy training ship. Cullen also had his own 'Skippers Quarters' which were carefully shut off from the rest of the house and consisted of two bedrooms, a living room and lounge. A secondary staircase led to the staff sleeping quarters.

The lounge-dining room on the ground floor features the beautiful maple panelling, glass doors and seating from the Second Class Drawing Room. With the original room being far too big, only half the fittings were used but despite this the end result is a perfectly balanced chamber. The installation has been cleverly done with the curvature of the ship still visible. The detail of the woodwork is also quite remarkable with gilded ribbons and swags. With regular polishing and treatment, the current owners have ensured that the condition of the panelling has not been allowed to deteriorate.

Poole Council approved the plans for the Boat House on 24th August 1936 and work commenced soon afterwards using a local builder supervised by Bartlett. Because it was built on a sand dune, a concrete platform was put down using very large aggregate. Tom Cullen also hired Alfred (Alf) Thomas Hatchard (1886-1965) to manage the house and look after his boats. The Hatchard family had a long association with boating and yachts in the Poole area and Alf was one of the few survivors from the Bowring Red Cross liner *Florizel* (3,081/1909) which sank off the coast of Newfoundland on 23rd February 1918. He had been a Royal Navy gunner aboard the ship which was carrying 138 passengers and crew from St John's to New York when she hit a reef near Cape Race during a storm with the loss of 94 lives. Alf and his wife Alice moved into the Boat House in 1936 and were joined by their six-year old grandson Keith whose father was in the Royal Navy submarine service. In later years, Keith wrote an evocative account of life at the Boat House during the 1930s and 1940s.

When Keith first arrived at the house, the landscaping of the garden was underway and men were French polishing the *Mauretania* woodwork. On the seaward side, a lily pond had been constructed whilst a small lawn ran out to a little headland. On this stood a sundial with the inscription *'Time, Tide and Starter wait for no man'*. The Boat House in those days was very much a male preserve and it is believed that Tom Cullen's wife never came down from Tyrrell's Wood to see the place. His son Peter, born in 1923, however, regularly stayed during school holidays and spent many a happy day messing around with boats and paddling his Red Indian-style canoe around Poole Harbour.

Cullen's weekend sailing parties usually consisted of around ten friends or business associates. As well as sailing, they also enjoyed fishing trips. The first of the fishing boats was *Iris I*, a converted lifeboat, which was believed to have come from Cunard Line's *Berengaria*. She was replaced by a second and more powerful diesel-launch called *Iris II*, which was built at Sandbanks by the boatbuilder Randalls. After a long day on the water, the party returned to the Boat House for a hearty meal prepared by Mrs. Hatchard. The evenings would usually be spent chatting or playing billiards on the three-quarter-size billiard table in the lounge-dining room.

On the 3rd September 1939 the tranquil life at the Boat House was shattered when war was declared against Germany. Only 66 miles from the French coast, Poole and its large harbour was strategically important during the Second World War. Shortly after the outbreak of the conflict Poole became the main base for international flights from Britain with the move by Imperial Airways of its flying boat operation from Hythe, Southampton. The Royal Navy and Royal Air Force soon followed. In June 1940 some of the troops evacuated from Dunkirk were billeted in the boat shed. The Boat House was especially vulnerable in the early years of the war. A large underground oil storage depot had been built into the hillside above the lake, only a short distance from the house. On 3rd June 1942 during one of the largest German air raids on Poole, an oil tank was destroyed by a bomb and a million gallons of aviation fuel spilled onto Lake Drive and the surrounding sand dunes. Fortunately, the prompt action of the fire brigade prevented any explosion and almost a fifth of the leaked fuel was salvaged. During the same raid, an unexploded 500lb bomb landed at the bottom of the garden of the Boat House and the Hatchard family was moved to a house near Hamworthy railway station.

On 29th June 1942 the Boat House and the area around Lake Drive was requisitioned as part of a Royal Air Force flying boat base, *RAF Hamworthy*. This was the main base for the Royal Australian Air Force 461 Squadron, which flew Sunderland flying boats on anti-submarine missions in the Atlantic. Later transferred from Coastal Command to Transport Command, the base ceased to exist on 1st May 1944 after it was handed over to the Royal Navy. As a Royal Navy establishment, *HMS Turtle*, it played a key role in the planning and training of personnel for the D-Day Landings. An observation post with a light anti-aircraft gun was mounted on the Boat House roof and the house was used, just prior to the 6th June 1944 invasion, for briefing landing craft commanders about the landings in Normandy. Closed after the war, the former naval base was reactivated in 1954 when it was taken over by the Royal Marines for training landing craft personnel. As the Amphibious School, Royal Marines, it remains in operation today, with its landing craft a regular sight in Poole Bay.

The Boat House was handed back to Tom Cullen in 1945 and the property soon returned to its pre-war glory with *Emily II* racing once again. In 1947 Cullen bought *Anne Marie*, a beautiful 1911-built ketch which had a teak hull with oak frames. By now, however, he was suffering from arthritis and his declining health forced him to give up the Boat House. On the 27th September 1951 it was sold at auction by Fox and Sons. In the meantime, he generously rewarded his loyal stalwart and sailing companion Alf Hatchard with not only his 1936 Lanchester car but also his fishing boat *Iris II*. The final chapter in the lives of these two gentlemen came in 1965, the year they both died.

As for the Boat House, the current owners have managed to maintain the atmosphere of a bygone era, not only of the 1930s but also of the Edwardian splendour of Cunard's most famous liner. Still a private house, the Boat House is only occasionally open to visitors.

The eminent architect Sir Hugh Casson (1910-1999) was a frequent visitor to the Boat House and produced this amusing sketch of *Mauretania* at anchor. Sir Hugh was involved in the interior designs for the P&O liner *Canberra* and the Royal Yacht *Britannia*. *[Zogolovitch Collection]*

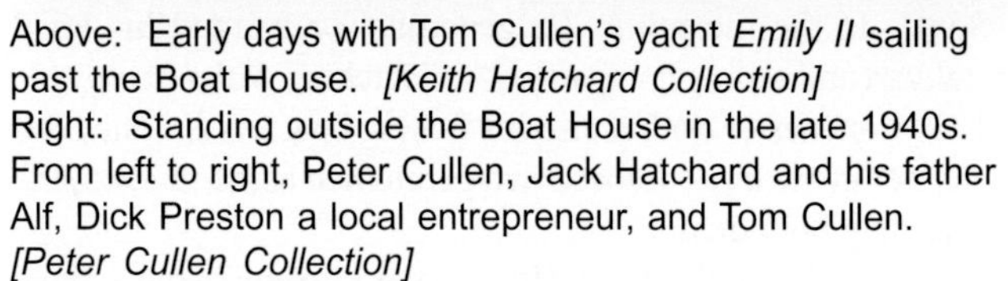

Above: Early days with Tom Cullen's yacht *Emily II* sailing past the Boat House. *[Keith Hatchard Collection]*
Right: Standing outside the Boat House in the late 1940s. From left to right, Peter Cullen, Jack Hatchard and his father Alf, Dick Preston a local entrepreneur, and Tom Cullen. *[Peter Cullen Collection]*
Below: Little has changed apart from the greenery.

The Second Class Drawing Room. *[Zogolovitch Collection]*

A corner of the downstairs room with original seat, ceiling and light fittings, and right, one of the free-standing columns.

The three bedrooms leading off the upper level include various *Mauretania* fixtures and fittings from the officers' cabins. The drawers beneath the bunks had uniquely-designed handles for ease of opening whilst at a sea.

The dressing chest-of-drawers and mirror in the captain's bedroom. *[Zogolovitch Collection]*

Below: The captain's dressing chest-of-drawers in the Boat House.
Right: To ensure that fittings were in the right place, the back of every item of furniture and panelling was marked in pencil, even one of the small top drawer of this chest.

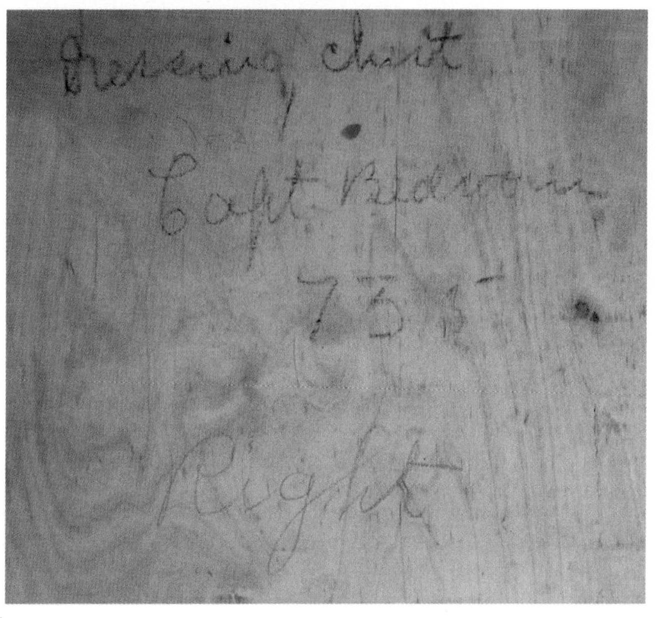

The Second Class Drawing Room entrance doors. *[Zogolovitch Collection]*

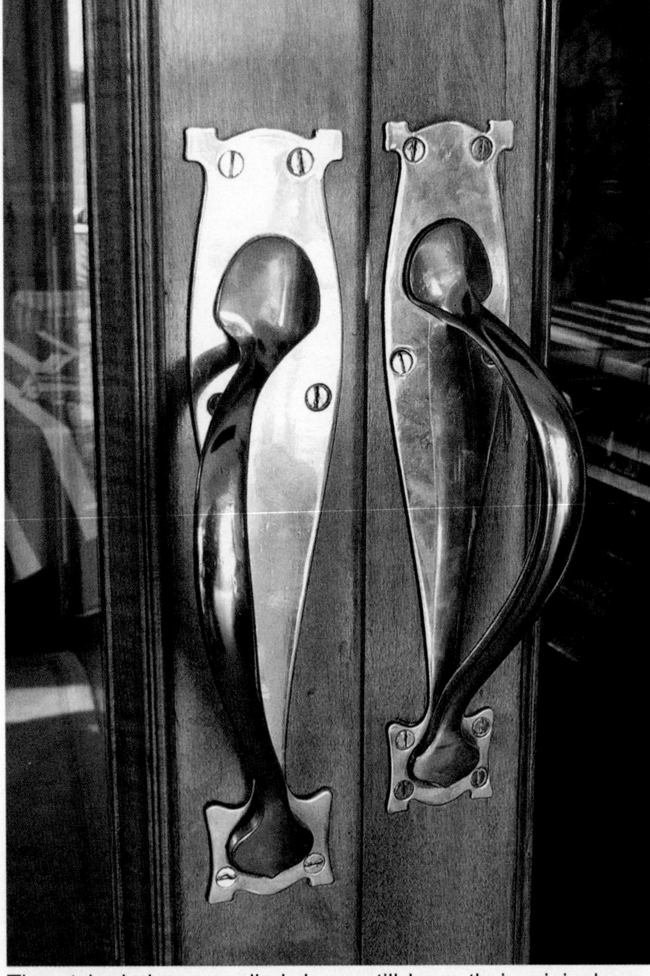

The etched-glass-panelled doors still have their original handles and hinges.

The remarkable detail of the maple woodwork. The gilded X-shaped ribbon feature was used throughout the ship and was based on ancient Roman designs.

The *Mauretania* weather vane at the top of the flagpole.

THE MAURETANIA, BRISTOL

The Avery family has been associated with the Bristol wine trade for almost two hundred years.

In 1865 John Avery bought a small retail wine business. Founded in 1793, this firm and its adjoining pub were situated near Bristol Cathedral, at the corner of Park Street and Frog Lane, in what is now 7-11 Park Street. Not long afterwards a road bridge was built over Frog Lane, turning Park Street into a major thoroughfare between Bristol town centre and the suburb of Clifton. John Avery used this opportunity to construct a large new building on the site of the old premises. Designed in a classical Greek style by the Bristol architect Henry Masters, this imposing four-storey building with a pub at street level and a large basement area was completed in 1870. By now John Avery's three sons John Clarke, Edwin and Joseph were all working for the company and continued to do so after his death in 1882.

The family-run concern flourished during the late 19th and early 20th centuries, mainly because of the success of the pub business. After the First World War, Ronald Avery, son of Joseph, joined the firm and soon made his mark as a wine connoisseur. Under his guidance, Avery's became well known as a fine wine specialist. Ronald bought well in the 1920s, especially red wines from Bordeaux, and these paid dividends during the lean vintage years of the next decade.

In 1934 Bristol City Council put forward plans to build a large new Council House on nearby College Green and it looked as if the Averys' building would have to be partially demolished to provide access to the new centre. After lengthy discussions an alternative road route was accepted. Despite opposition from his father, Ronald put in hand an ambitious redevelopment plan for 7-11 Park Street which included the refurbishment of the existing premises plus the building of an extension to the rear which would include a large entertainment complex with bars and dining area.

The *Mauretania* Grand Staircase panelling bought at the May 1935 auction was put into storage at the company's warehouse in Culver Street and in October 1936 Averys obtained more *Mauretania* items, via Frederick Bartlett, from the liquidated Mauretania Syndicate, including the First Class Lounge panels, pillars and chandeliers plus the dome from the First Class Library. So many *Mauretania* items were incorporated into the new building that when it completed in December 1938, it was called The Mauretania.

The Mauretania consisted of six bars and lounges situated mainly on the Park Street ground floor (Upper Deck Bar, Grill Room, Mauretania Lounge and Sun Lounge) and the lower ground floor which was appropriately called the Lower Deck. The architect for the rear extension and interior design was W. H. Watkins from Bristol, who specialised in designing cinemas. His cinema-style can be seen throughout the Mauretania building, especially the St. Georges Road entrance that led to the Lower Deck, Mauretania and Sun Lounge on the first floor. The main entrance for the Upper Deck bar was on Park Street whilst the Lower Deck could be accessed from either side of the building at St. Georges Road or Frog Lane. Frog Lane was the main entrance for the Grill Room although this could also be entered via another entrance on St. Georges Road.

The Upper and Lower Deck bars featured not only the large figured walnut panels from the Grand Staircase but also many of the fine small panels and balustrades which were incorporated into the bar counters. Above the fireplace in the Lower Deck Bar were the beautifully carved panels which were originally behind the large, recessed settee in the First Class Grand Entrance on A Deck. Another exceptionally fine settee from the Upper C Deck entrance can be found to one side of the bar area.

Behind the Upper Deck Bar was the Mauretania Lounge with the glass dome from the First Class Library and a number of free-standing columns from the Grand Staircase. This lounge led to the Sun Lounge at the rear of the building with views of old Bristol Docks in the distance and a long colonnaded building in the square below. Now called Brunel House, this had been completed in 1839 as the Royal Western Hotel for one of the first regular transatlantic services run by the Great Western Steamship Company and its Brunel-designed *Great Western*. The Bristol-New York service was short-lived and in 1843 *Great Western*'s home port became Liverpool. Despite this setback, the hotel continued until 1855.

The jewel in the crown of The Mauretania is what remains of *Mauretania*'s First Class Lounge in the Grill Room and its small adjoining chamber on Park Street. The Grill Room itself consisted of the mahogany panelling, the ram's head fluted columns, six of the elaborate cut crystal electric ceiling lights and the twin pair of entrance doors, each with a fancy 'M' for *Mauretania*. Separated by another room with panelling from the Grand Staircase is a charming room with more tall columns and the panels from around the First Class Lounge marble fireplace. The fireplace itself is, however, not from *Mauretania*. Above the door is the famous Cunard crowned lion holding a globe whilst standing on a rope. This room was originally the Avery wine and liquor shop with its plastered ceiling featuring large letter As representing the Avery name.

The Mauretania also has a surprising connection with another great transatlantic liner, which too had been the largest ship in the world. The 60,000-ton *Leviathan* started life as *Vaterland*, the second of three giant liners built just before the 1914-1918 war for Hamburg-Amerikanische-Packetfahrt-Actien-Gesellschaft (Hapag). This trio, ordered in 1910, was Germany's answer to White Star Line's three *Olympic*-class ships under construction at Belfast. At the end of the First World War , the Treaty of Versailles imposed incredible hardship on the German nation and devastated the once great German merchant navy. All vessels over 1,600-tons were handed to the Allies including Hapag's giants which became Cunard Line's *Berengaria* (ex *Imperator*); White Star's *Majestic* (ex *Bismarck*) and the newly-established United States Line's *Leviathan* (ex *Vaterland*). *Leviathan* was sold for scrap in 1938 to Metal Industries and another Hampton's auction was held in March 1938 to sell its fixtures and fittings. Ronald Avery purchased a number of items in this sale including six of the first class iron lift gates, two of which are still in use as entrances on the Park Street side of The Mauretania. He also bought a number of tables, chairs and sofas from the main First Class Lounge and these were used in the Grill Room. The railing in the stair well leading from Frog Lane to the Grill Room incorporated the ornate metal rails and clock from the upper balcony of *Leviathan*'s First Class Dining Saloon. In 1938, Avery obtained from his friend Robert McCrone the bell from the sunken German battleship *Grosser Kurfürst*. This originally stood in the Sun Lounge and is now in the possession of the Avery family.

The Mauretania soon became one of Bristol's best known landmarks with its neon light, one of the first in the city, showing *Mauretania* moving through the water. Its elegant interior was also a great draw with meals served by waiters in white tuxedoes with white gloves. This success was cut short by the Second World War. Like most of Britain's major seaports, Bristol suffered considerable damage during German air raids. In 78 air raids on the city much of the old city was ruined, with almost five thousand inhabitants either wounded or killed. Miraculously, The Mauretania survived unscathed despite 23 incendiary bombs landing on its reinforced roof in one night and which were lobbed over the side by the alert fire-watching team. The local Cunard White Star Line office at 65 Baldwin Street was not so lucky and was destroyed. Cunard Line had been in Bristol since 1916 when it bought The Royal Line, which operated a fortnightly passenger-mail service between Bristol and Canada. In September 1949, *Mauretania* was once more associated with Cunard when the company opened a new booking office in The Mauretania. This later became the Cunard-owned travel agent Brocklebank Travel until its closure in 1980 when its place was taken by the Avery wine shop.

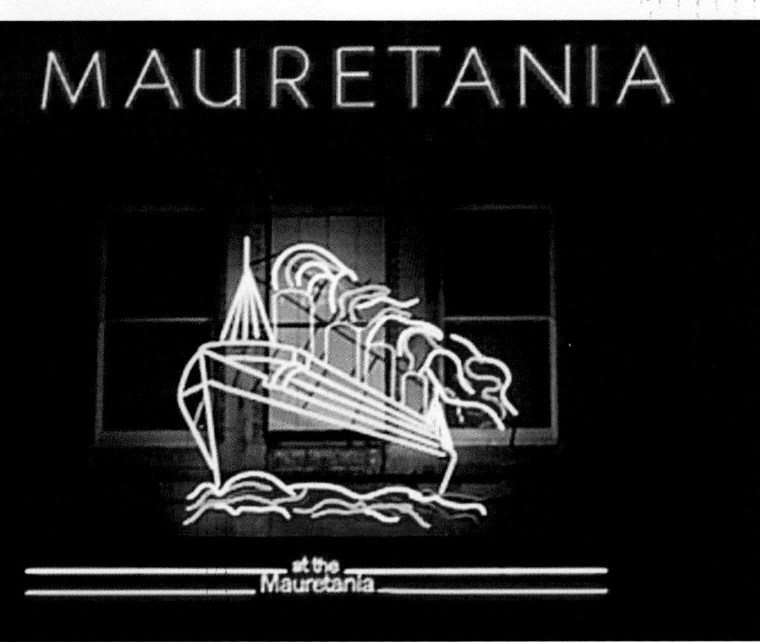

The neon sign, one of the first in Bristol, was fitted in 1937.
[Pml Signs]

Despite the bombing and devastation in Bristol, The Mauretania was a popular venue for service personnel on leave, especially Americans. After the war the area around Park Street became rundown and although Avery's expanded its wine business, The Mauretania never recovered its pre-war glory. By the early 1960s, the Lower Deck had become a bierkeller run by Lowenbrau and in 1969 an attempt was made by a company called Philander Inns Ltd. to revitalise The Mauretania's flagging fortunes. Whilst the former Grill Room remained a restaurant, the Upper Deck bar was transformed into a nautically-themed bar, The Admiral's Bar, complete with cannon, ship's wheel, portrait of Admiral Nelson and red plush seating. It also had a nautical sound-track of waves, gulls, 21-gun salutes and ships' bells! This venture closed in 1976 after a serious fire destroyed the Sun Lounge and smoke damaged much of the panelling and gilt-work in the Grill Room. The panels in the glass dome of the Mauretania Lounge were also ruined. This was the year in which Ronald Avery died and the business was taken over by his son John, who is one of Britain's leading wine experts and the 2004-5 Master of The Vintners Company in London.

In the late 1970s The Mauretania reopened for business as the Pinafore Wine Bar and Mauretania Brasserie. Featured on the outside of the building were the original port side brass *Mauretania* letters which had been sold in Southampton at the 22nd October 1936 liquidation sale of The Mauretania Syndicate. Obtained by the then tenant of the bar and restaurant, Stephen Samuel, they were later taken down and stored within the building. The bierkeller had been renamed King Dick and in 1983 the lease-holding for the former Lower Deck was taken over by the brewer Eldridge Pope.

Also in 1983, the building was sold to a property company and for more than 20 years attempts have been made to regenerate the business, most of which have ended in failure. After the closure of The Mauretania Wine Bar, 7-11 Park Street was declared a Grade II listed building on 26th August 1994 by what is now English Heritage, to preserve the unique interiors. However, despite this preservation order, the panelling and fittings have had mixed fortunes during the past decade, especially during the period of the Met Club and Bar which came to an end in 2003. The former Upper Deck Bar has now been transformed into Bar III, whilst the former Grill Room has become a members-only club and the Mauretania Lounge, a discotheque. Much of the panelling has also been restored and the Lower Deck has been completely refurbished and is now Vibes, a gay night club. Unfortunately, during this latest transformation all the remaining panelling and free-standing columns in the discotheque have been removed. The set of electric lights in the Grill Room have also been replaced with modern lighting which has ruined the unique aspect of this room, which had remained unchanged since 1938.

Meanwhile, Avery's continue to operate an impressive wine cellar from its premises in Culver Street. The Avery link with *Mauretania*, however, ceased in 1985 when the dome above the lift on A Deck was disposed of whilst unused panels from *Mauretania*, which had been in store since 1938, were sold to a furniture maker.

This is not the end of The Mauretania Bristol story. On 9th June 2000 an auction of surplus farm machinery, building materials, architectural salvage and household furniture was held by Tayler and Fletcher at the Great Tew Estate, Oxfordshire. Among the numerous architectural relics were about 30 lots from *Mauretania* including figured walnut panels from the Grand Staircase. These not only had the lot number 1613 from the May 1935 sale written on the backs but also on an original Hampton's label. Lot 1613 was of course the Grand Staircase bought by Ronald Avery on day four of the great sale. How these came to be at Great Tew is unclear. However, what is certain is they were the remnants not used in the fitting out of The Mauretania in Bristol. Most of the panelling was bought by an antique dealer from Hartley Wintney, Hampshire who plans to incorporate them into his house. He also acquired part of the white enamelled wooden First Class Library ceiling and a cornice from an alcove in the First Class Lounge.

The neon light design was also used in this glazed pottery mug produced for Avery's in the late 1930s.

The rather austere 1870-building on Park Street with its 1930s extension at the rear. Note the distinctive Mauretania neon light showing the ship and her name.

The May 1935 purchases were originally stored in Avery's Culver Street warehouse, which was not far from Park Street. In the photo below, Ronald Avery is second from the left. Lot 1604 was the port side walnut panelling from the Grand Entrance on Upper C Deck. The beautifully carved, recessed centre for a settee (above) was also from the Upper C Deck entrance. The gentleman to the right of Ronald Avery is holding a door from the vestibule leading onto the A Deck promenade - see photo bottom right. *[Top and bottom left: John Avery Collection; bottom right: Paul Louden-Brown Collection]*

MUSICAL PROGRAMME

by Miss Eileen Vaughan, Messrs. Dave Llewellyn
Leslie Groves and Alfred Parkman

Dinner

ON THE OCCASION OF
THE COMPLETION OF THE

"Mauretania"

BRISTOL

NINETEENTH DECEMBER 1938

A dinner was given on 19th December 1938 to celebrate the completion of The Mauretania. Although the meal served was rather rich for today's taste, the choice of wines and drinks was very impressive. *[John Avery Collection]*

MENU	*WINES*
Cornish No. 2 Oysters	Sylvia Amontillado Verzenay 1928
English Melon	
Sole Colbert	Schloss Johannisberg Cabinet (*orig. abf. Prince von Metternich*)
Pigeon Bordelaise	Clos Fourtet 1924 (*Ch. Bottled*)
"Friday, 19th Dec., 1856: We are now half loaded, or rather over"—*Extract from John Jellard's Journal of Voyage of the Barque "Avery."*	
Boiled Turkey with Chestnut Sauce Braised Celery, Potato Croquettes	Chateau Haut Brion 1920 (*Ch. Bottled*) Grands Echezeaux 1915
Punch à la Romaine	
Braised York Ham, Champagne Sauce	
Dessert	Bristol Milk Sandeman 1904 Ferreira 1896 Special Reserve 1878
Coffee	

The Grand Entrance on A Deck. *[Zogolovitch Collection]*

The bar of the Upper Deck in 1938 incorporated panels from the staircase and carved ribbon panels above the starboard and port sides of the entrance hall. Apart from a few carved shields, most of these have now gone. *[John Avery Collection]*

However, there are still a number of walnut panels from the stairwells, with simple but elegant carved pilasters featuring the leaf pattern used on the free-standing columns in the Grand Entrance.

The dome from the First Class Library (left) was incorporated into the Mauretania Lounge, which was behind the Upper Deck bar. The dome was lit by lights attached to columns from the Grand Entrance. *[Paul Louden-Brown Collection]*

Middle and bottom right: Mauretania Lounge in 1938. *[John Avery Collection]*

Left: Damaged by fire in 1976, all that remains of the original dome is the metal frame.

At the entrance to the Mauretania Lounge stood a Moorish-style fireplace which was not from *Mauretania*. This was flanked by wooden columns, which once stood either side of the A Deck elevator. *[John Avery Collection]*

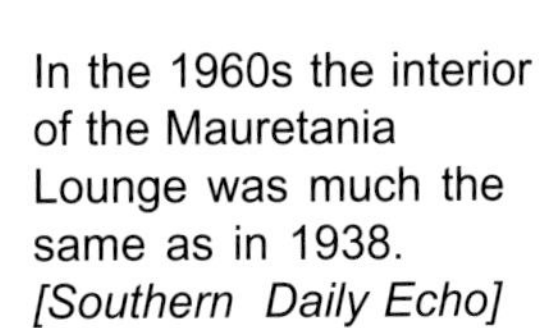

In the 1960s the interior of the Mauretania Lounge was much the same as in 1938. *[Southern Daily Echo]*

After the 1976 fire the seating was removed and the area became a discotheque. The fireplace was replaced with art nouveau tiled-panels, although the panels and columns remained in place and were still there when the building was given in 1994 a Grade II listing intended to preserve for posterity its unique interiors. Despite this preservation order, the last remaining panels and columns in the discotheque have been removed and unceremoniously 'stored' in one of the lower level mezzanine floors at 7-11 Park Street.

In 1938 the beautiful, carved panels from behind the recessed settee in the Grand Entrance on A Deck (bottom left) were above the fireplace in the Lower Deck of The Mauretania. These are now probably hidden behind panelling, whilst the settee from Upper C Deck (see page 103) is protected by an enormous leopard's skin, curved seat. (middle and bottom right) *[Left and middle left: John Avery Collection; Bottom left: Tyne & Wear Archives]*

Mauretania's First Class Lounge in 1907. *[Zogolovitch Collection]*

The Mauretania's Grill Room in 1938. This contained many of the First Class Lounge fixtures and fittings bought in 1936 from the liquidators of The Mauretania Syndicate. However, the tables, chairs and settees came from *Leviathan*'s First Class Lounge. *[John Avery Collection]*

Above each of the entrance doors is the letter M for *Mauretania*. Note the original door hinges and, reflected in the glass, the cut crystal electric ceiling lights. Despite the Grade II listing, these lights have been removed whilst the white ceiling has been painted green.

Between the two doors are two mirrored panels. These were originally windows in one of the curved First Class Lounge alcoves, which overlooked the Boat Deck Promenade. *[Left: Zogolovitch Collection]*

More of the First Class Lounge can be found in what was in 1938 (left), the Avery wine and liquor shop. Note the A for Avery. *[John Avery Collection]*

Above, below and overleaf: The detail of the carving and metalwork is breathtaking with ram's head columns, a Cunard lion above the door, oak leaves with acorns in the mirror surround and X-shaped ribbons on the handles and column bases.

A number of items from United States Line's *Leviathan* (ex-*Vaterland*) have ended up in The Mauretania. The ornate railing from the upper gallery of the First Class Dining Saloon was used as the banister-rail in the stair well, which linked the Grill Room and the Frog Lane entrance. The clock was also from the First Class Dining Saloon. The stairwell was demolished and all that remains of the railing is one small section. The whereabouts of the clock remains a mystery. *[Top: Peter Newall Collection; bottom left: John Avery Collection]*

Six of *Leviathan*'s lift gates were used in The Mauretania. A pair was inside the building leading to the upper levels. *[John Avery Collection]*

Two lift gates are on the outside of the building whilst another pair, which was once inside, is now in the Avery cellar across the road (bottom left).

One of the remaining tables from *Leviathan*'s First Class Lounge.

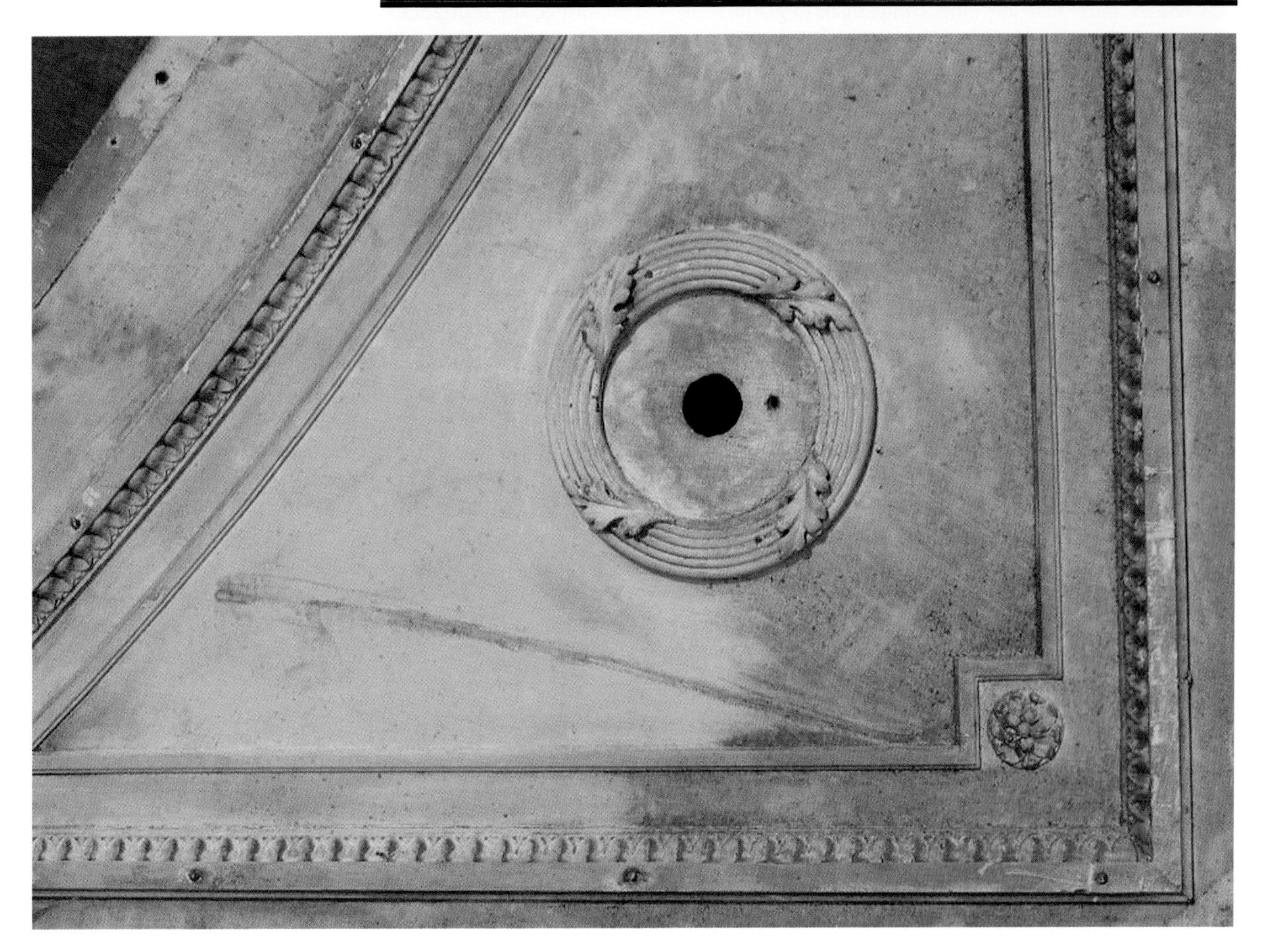

Some of the former items from The Mauretania, Bristol bought at the Great Tew Estate auction in June 2000. Unlike the panelling, which has survived at The Mauretania, these panels from the Grand Staircase (Lot 1613) have not been overpolished and remain in excellent condition. This section of the white enamelled wooden First Class Library ceiling also has the maker's mark of C. Mellier and Co. on the reverse. *[Adam Gratwick]*

PINEWOOD STUDIOS

Situated not far from London and close to the M25 motorway, Pinewood Studios is one of the most famous film studios in the world. In its seventy years of existence, hundreds of classic films have been made here including many in the James Bond and Carry on series.

It all started on the 25th September 1934 when Charles Boot (1874-1945), head of the Sheffield-based construction firm Henry Boot and Son, bought at auction an 158-acre estate called Heatherden Hall at Iver Heath, Buckinghamshire. Charles was the eldest son of Henry Boot who founded his building firm in 1886. During the first two decades of the 20th century, the company obtained a number of large government contracts including the Calshot Seaplane Base, Southampton and Manston Aerodrome in Kent. By the 1930s it had built 35,000 new homes, more than any other company in England.

Heatherden Hall had been owned by a Canadian financier and Member of Parliament for Brentford and Chiswick, Lt. Col. Grant Morden. He bought the 19th century house and grounds from K.S. Ranjitsinhji, Indian prince and famous cricketer who played for Sussex and England and who later became the Maharajah of Nawangar. Morden spent £300,000 transforming the estate and hall with the addition of a large ballroom and one of the first indoor swimming pools in a British privately owned house. In the extensive grounds and gardens he built tennis and squash courts and an ornamental lake spanned by a balustraded bridge. With its close proximity to London, Heatherden Hall became a popular weekend retreat for politicians and statesmen. It was here that the Irish Free-State treaty was signed on the 6th December 1921. At the auction run by Goddard and Smith, Charles Boot paid £35,000 for Heatherden Hall, a fraction of the amount Morden lavished on the house and gardens. The estate became a country club with the ballroom turned into the main restaurant.

For some time Charles Boot had the idea of building a major film studio in Britain, which would rival those in the United States. In the early 1930s London had around 20 film studios, most rather small and disorganised. With his purchase of the Iver Heath estate, Boot decided in 1935 to build five state-of-the-art stages at the rear of the main house, which would cost over a £1 million. He invited the mill owner Joseph Arthur Rank and a wealthy widow, Lady Yule, to join him in the new company, which was called Pinewood Studios Ltd., a name inspired by the large number of pine trees in the grounds. Thus one of the best-known British film studios was born and with the incorporation of the *Mauretania* fittings, the great liner would once again play host to the rich and famous.

The son of a millionaire flour miller, Joseph Arthur Rank (1888-1972), later Lord Rank, was a devout Methodist. He was also a Sunday school teacher and found that screening religious films got a better response than lectures. In 1933 he formed the Religious Film Society and his first film ran for twenty minutes and cost £2,700. The following year he founded a religious film company, British National Films, with the young producer John Corfield and Lady Yule, a rather eccentric but extremely wealthy woman, who saw films as an opportunity to promote the British way of life. British National's first full length feature 'Turn of the Tide' struggled to get a decent film distribution in Britain. So Rank decided to form his own distribution company. General Film Distributors, which had as its logo, the now famous 'man with a gong' which later became the trade mark for Rank films. A natural film producer and businessman, J. Arthur Rank eventually took control of Pinewood Studios and his company grew into the giant Rank Organisation.

Annie, Lady Yule was an interesting character who had been left a fortune (estimates vary between eight and fifteen million pounds) after the death in 1928 of her husband Sir David Yule (1858-1928), a Calcutta-based merchant and banker who owned the Daily Chronicle newspaper. Lady Yule also ran an Arab horse stud. In 1930 she took delivery of one of the finest yachts of the time. Built on the Clyde by John Brown and Co., the 1,582-ton, 300-foot, twin-screw, turbine-driven *Nahlin* was sold in 1937 to the Romanian Government

Lady Yule's yacht, the *Nahlin,* dressed overall in the Mersey.. *[J. & M. Clarkson Collection]*

as a Royal Yacht. *Nahlin* returned to Britain in 1999. After a period of lay-up at Liverpool, she was taken to Germany in 2005 for restoration by the leading yacht builder, HDW Nobiskrug.

Construction work on Pinewood Studios started in December 1935 and the new complex was officially opened by Dr. Leslie Burgin, Parliamentary Secretary of the Board of Trade, on 30th September 1936. As well as the film stages, a large administration block was built behind the old Heatherden Hall. This had 65 offices including special suites for producers. The main entrance to the administration block provides a taster of *Mauretania*'s presence at Pinewood. Surrounded by an immense wooden Elizabethan carving taken from Allum Hall in Derbyshire, is the first of two pairs of large 7-foot high oak doors from the upper First Class Dining Saloon. These are part of the items bought by Charles Boot from the bankrupt Mauretania Syndicate in 1936 to supplement his original May 1935 purchases. These doors lead into a two-storey high entrance hall. At the opposite end is another pair of glass-panelled swing doors leading into the garden. These came from the First Class Library.

On the second floor the Executive Boardroom contains most of *Mauretania*'s First Class Library with its Hepplewhite-style panels of polished sycamore. Apart from the dome, which is in The Mauretania, Bristol, the scene is so complete that one can imagine being aboard the ship. The seven electric cut crystal ceiling lights have been restored whilst the bookcases are filled with books behind brass mesh grilles. At either end of the room are alcoves, which once contained the curtained windows that looked out on to the promenade deck. Here the original curtain cords and wood curtain-runners remain undisturbed whilst the entrance swing doors with bevelled glass and gilt ormolu rails, are still in regular use. These doors received special mention in the 1907 *Mauretania* commemorative issue of 'The Shipbuilder'. As for the woodwork, the delicately carved detail is very impressive, especially the gilt frieze of oak leaves and tiny acorns running along the round-headed main doors of the bookcases.

The real surprise at Pinewood, however, lies in the 150-foot long picture gallery, which links the old house to the administration block. Displayed along the walls are photographs of scenes from some of Pinewood's most famous films. These are separated by sixteen of the original *fleur de pêche* lilac-coloured marble pilasters from the First Class Lounge for which Charles Boot paid £4-15s a pair. The barrel vaulted roof, meanwhile, comes from the glass panelled roof of the Smoke Room whilst at either end of the long gallery are Frank Murray's long-forgotten semi-circular paintings 'Old New York' and 'Old Liverpool'. The former clearly shows a paddle steamer with a large United States flag on the stern and below each painting are two pairs of rams-head columns from the First Class Lounge. As Captain Rostron would probably have passed under these paintings on numerous occasions, it is appropriate that the classic British film *'A Night to Remember'* was filmed at Pinewood in 1957. This film was about the *Titanic* disaster of 1912 when Captain Rostron was in command of the Cunard liner *Carpathia*, which rescued many of the survivors.

The swing door at the far end of the corridor is another from the Upper First Class Dining Saloon and it is a tribute to the quality of the Edwardian craftsmanship that the original hinges are still in place after almost a hundred years of constant use.

The old Heatherden Hall also incorporates a number of *Mauretania* items. The house is entered through two pairs of walnut doors with ornate chased brass handles. These were from the First Class Smoke Room. In the former ballroom, now a restaurant, are the upper parts of two intricately carved curved oak screens which once stood in the lower section of the two-deck First Class Dining Saloon. Meanwhile, the pair of doors leading from the restaurant into the bar is the second set of oak doors from the First Class Dining Saloon.

Despite being part of a busy studio complex for 70 years, the *Mauretania* material is in excellent condition and well maintained. Unfortunately, for security reasons, the *Mauretania* areas at Pinewood are not open to the public.

The 158-acre Pinewood Studios is situated in the midst of beautiful English countryside. The original house, Heatherden Hall (front right), faces gardens, a lake and woodland. Behind it is the long administration block, most of which was built in the 1930s. The studio complex includes numerous film facilities, including the immense 007 Silent Stage (middle back) with its huge water tank, in which many of the James Bond scenes were shot, but which was damaged by fire in July 2006. Bottom left is the large open-air stage, which has also been used in the production of numerous famous films. *[Pinewood Studios Ltd.]*

Charles Boot (1874-1945), founder of Pinewood Studios.
[Henry Boot PLC]

The main entrance to the administration block consists of an immense Elizabethan carving with twisted columns.

The oak entrance doors are from *Mauretania*'s Upper First Class Dining Saloon (left). At the opposite end of the entrance hall, the glass-panelled swing doors leading into the garden are from the First Class Library.

The entrance to the old Heatherden Hall consists of two pairs of walnut doors from the First Class Smoke Room. They have their original chased brass handles and one set of doors is inlaid with the chain pattern in sycamore, which featured in many of the large panels of the Smoke Room.

Left: The 150-foot gallery which links the administration block to the old house has sections of the glass-vaulted roof from *Mauretania*'s First Class Smoke Room and at the opposite ends are the two well-known paintings which used to hang in the Smoke Room.

Below: 'Old New York'

Above: 'Old Liverpool'
Left and below: Fourteen of the 10-foot high lilac-coloured marble pilasters from the First Class Lounge line either side of the long gallery. The gilded carved capitals are quite remarkable and are similar to those found on the wooden columns and pilasters in other areas of the Lounge.

Apart from the dome, which is in The Mauretania, Bristol, the Executive Board Room at Pinewood Studios contains much of *Mauretania*'s First Class Library (left). The stained sycamore panelling is in excellent condition. The lights have been cleaned and it is hard to believe that they are 100 years old. The entrance doors with their original handles, hinges and fine bevelled glass, are also in regular use. *[Left: Zogolovitch Collection]*

As with most of Harold Peto's designs for *Mauretania*, it is the detail and wonderful craftsmanship which never fail to impress. To the right of the bookcase hangs a portrait of J. Arthur Rank, the driving force behind Pinewood Studios great success.

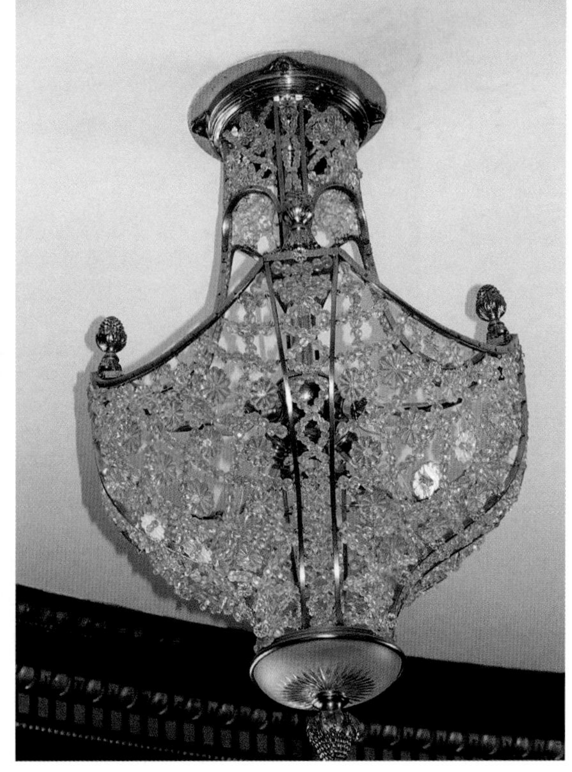

Two of the *Mauretania* gems at Pinewood are the sections of the oak screens, which once stood in the lower First Class Dining Room. Again, the detail of the carvings is astonishing with a cornucopia, pomegranate and intricate leaf patterns. The screens are in Pinewood's main restaurant, the location for a few films, including the 1982 'Who Dares Wins'.

THE OAST HOUSE, HILDENBORUGH

In 1965 a young couple, Kay and Roy Cope, fell in love with a dilapidated oast house and its ancient barn on Hilden Farm, Hildenborough, Kent. It was situated in an area that was once renowned for growing hops. Oast houses were used to dry the green hops. The circular buildings with their distinctive ventilator cowled roofs, which turn in the wind, were a common sight. As the hop industry declined many of the oast houses in Kent were converted into highly desirable residences. The Copes bought the property at auction for £4,500 and spent almost as much again over the next few years converting it into a delightful set of buildings.

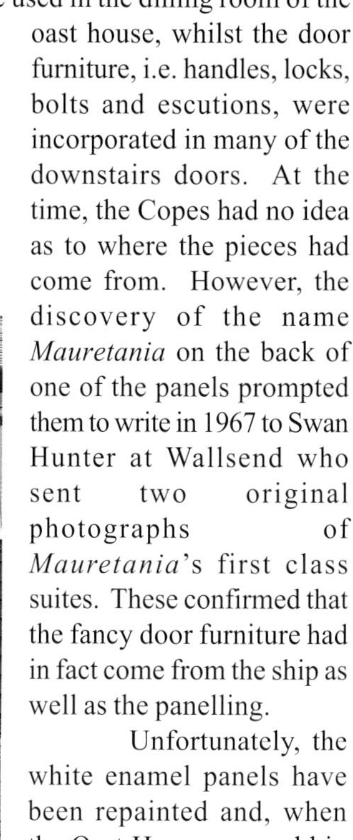

Kay and Roy Cope outside the Oast House.

In July 1966 the Copes visited the antique dealer A. Dall and Sons in Totland on the Isle of Wight. Here they found a large quantity of fine panelling, some painted, others made from maple, satinwood and mahogany. There were also doors, chests of drawers and bed ends, all from the First Class cabins aboard *Mauretania*. These had been bought in the 1935 auction by the Crinage family, owners of the 19th century Fort Redoubt, Freshwater Bay, which had been converted into a private residence. Until their purchase by Mr. Dall, they had been stored in one of the tunnels beneath the fort.

The Copes bought much of the panelling, door fittings and one of the magnificent satin wood chest of drawers. Some of the smaller items still had original Cunard luggage labels attached. E. Dibbens and Sons, Ryde transported the whole lot from the island to Hildenborough for £8. A number of the Adam-style white enamelled panels from cabins A8 and A12 were used in the dining room of the oast house, whilst the door furniture, i.e. handles, locks, bolts and escutions, were incorporated in many of the downstairs doors. At the time, the Copes had no idea as to where the pieces had come from. However, the discovery of the name *Mauretania* on the back of one of the panels prompted them to write in 1967 to Swan Hunter at Wallsend who sent two original photographs of *Mauretania*'s first class suites. These confirmed that the fancy door furniture had in fact come from the ship as well as the panelling.

Unfortunately, the white enamel panels have been repainted and, when the Oast House was sold in 2005, the new owners carefully removed the panels and placed them in storage. The removal has also revealed for the first time in almost forty years the lot numbers from the 1935 sale. As much of the spare maple and satinwood panels had been sold to an architectural reclamation company in June 2000, the brief association of the *Mauretania* with an oast house in Kent has almost been severed. The three-foot long cased model of *Mauretania*, which once was in the Oast House, however, now has pride of place in the Boat House at Hamworthy, Poole.

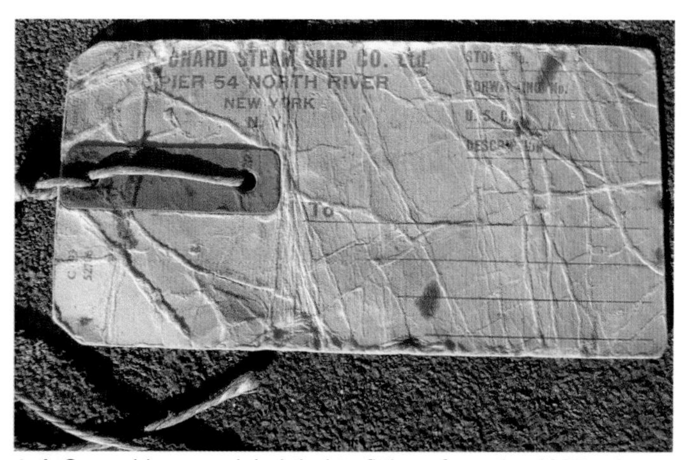

A Cunard luggage label tied to fittings from the 1935 sale.

The painted white enamel panels came from the Adam-style first class cabins A8 and A12, forward of the Library on A Deck. *[Right: Zogolovitch Collection]*

Unused first class cabin-door furniture. Even the door handles and escutcheons have the X-ribbon design. Right: classical details were also found on an item as small as a cupboard handle; in this case, a flaming torch.

A satinwood chest of drawers from one of the first class suites. The drawers fit perfectly and also feature *Mauretania*'s X-ribbon trademark on the handles.

The elegant shape of a cabin door handle.

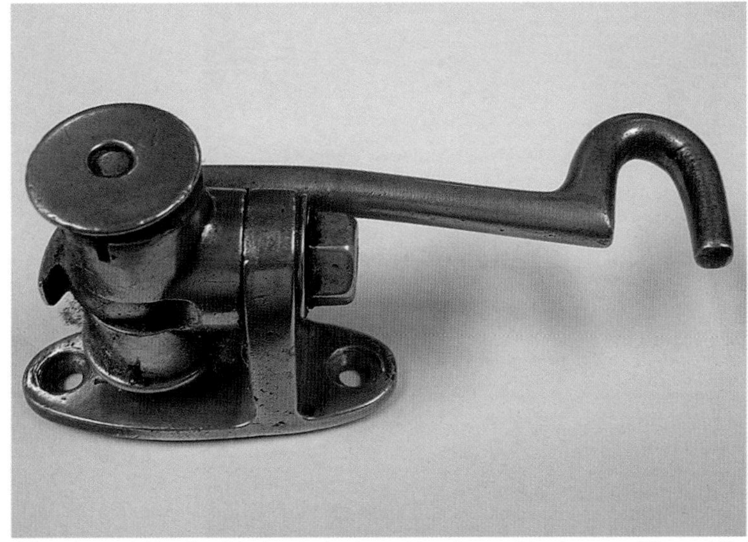

The clever 'silent' cabin hook designed to stop cabin doors rattling whilst underway.

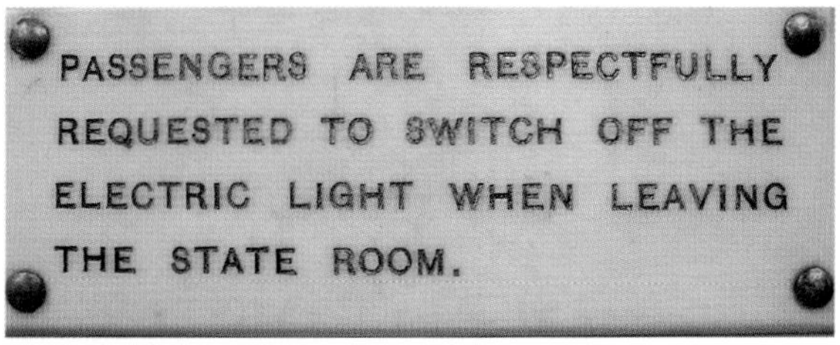

PASSENGERS ARE RESPECTFULLY REQUESTED TO SWITCH OFF THE ELECTRIC LIGHT WHEN LEAVING THE STATE ROOM.

A cabin notice made from ivorine, a type of plastic made to look like ivory.

THE NEW CHURCH, KENSINGTON

At a busy junction in the heart of the Westbourne Grove area of North Kensington, London stands a small church, which has a most unusual history. Despite its 18th century external appearance, the New Church at 5 Pembridge Villas was only completed in 1925. It is part of a Christian church founded in the City of London in 1787. Sometimes known as the New Jerusalem Church, its teachings are based on the theological writings of a Swedish philosopher, Emanuel Swedenborg.

The New Church in the 1920s. *[The New Church]*

The New Church first came to Kensington in 1872 when a wealthy benefactor bought an old Baptist church in Palace Gardens Terrace. However, by 1911 this building had become unsuitable and was sold. For the next 14 years Sunday worship took place in the nearby Lindsay Hall. In 1924 a replacement site was found at Pembridge Villas for a new place of worship and on 24th October the following year, the 'new' New Church was formally dedicated. The stained glass windows came from the old church whilst the chancel has as its centrepiece a painting of the Last Supper by the Victorian painter William Frederick Eames (1835-1918). His most famous painting was 'When did you last see your father?', which shows a scene from the English Civil War of a young boy in Royalist dress standing in front of a group of Commonwealth soldiers seated at a table. Interestingly, at 7 Pembridge Villas, next door to the New Church, lived another famous Victorian painter, William Frith. In the studio of this house he painted his 1852 masterpiece, 'Derby Day'.

In the early 1930s the church committee decided to set up a memorial fund in honour of its late Minister, Rev. James F. Buss. At the instigation of J. W. Jobson, a member of the church who was also the shipbroker for Metal Industries, it was decided to purchase a run of panelling at the May 1935 *Mauretania* auction. This would be used to refurbish the chancel. The church bought two lots of 11-foot high walnut panelling (lots 313 and 319), totalling 82 feet, from the port and starboard vestibules which linked the First Class Smoke Room and the First Class Lounge.

The church paid £43-1s for the panels and these were erected in the chancel by W.E. Tamlin and Son for £25. The new chancel, with its beautiful polished panelling, was dedicated at a well-attended service on 18th January 1936. In 1938 the remaining pieces of wood, including the doorframes, were used to refit the vestibule of the church. This work cost £103-4s and was also carried out by W.E. Tamlin and Son.

The woodwork in the New Church has been very well cared for over the years and this haven of peace, which is usually open during the week, is well worth a visit.

The walnut panels around the chancel.

THE WHITE HOUSE, POOLE

Many of the finest cabins aboard *Mauretania* were situated on B Deck where the corridors were panelled in dark polished mahogany. These panels were 6 feet 11inches high with dentil cornice mouldings, broken by Ionic-capital pilasters decorated with ribbon and husk pendants. The overall effect was of great confidence and strength. During the May 1935 auction, the panelling was sold in thirteen lots, each consisting of at least 100 feet in length. Walter Martin bought seven lots totalling over 800 feet. Some of this panelling was re-erected in Sheds 14-16, Southampton Docks. Its whereabouts and the rest of this rare panelling is anyone's guess but probably ended up in a hotel reception and ground floor area like the Mon Ami Hotel in St. Michael Road, West Cliff, Bournemouth. Apparently, the owners at the time were from India and wanted the hotel to be themed along the lines of India during the British Raj so the mahogany panels were perfect for the job. However, during the early 1980s, with their provenance long-since forgotten, the panels were ripped out during a refurbishment of the ground floor. They were piled up in the forecourt ready to be burned but the hotel's carpenter recognised the quality of the wood and rediscovered its origin. He took it home and sometime later he sold the lot for £70 to the owner of a large house in Canford Cliffs, Poole called the White House. The carpenter also fitted it in the dining room where it remains to this day.

Some of the panels re-erected in Southampton in 1935. *[Zogolovitch Collection]*

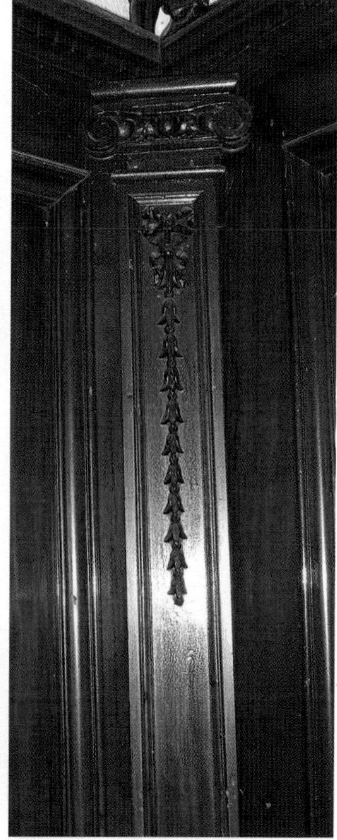

The dining room of the White House

SOUTHAMPTON GIRLS' GRAMMAR SCHOOL

The Southampton Grammar School for Girls in Hill Lane, used to have over 100 feet of *Mauretania*'s first class mahogany panelling lining the main entrance to the school and adjoining foyer, which was also called the crush hall. Soon after the foundation stone of the new school building was laid on 1st June 1935, the architect Mr. Hollis announced in the school magazine that the panelling had been acquired for the school. It is possible that this was from Walter Martin or one of the other buyers who purchased this section of the ship, including Ronald Avery or Charles Boot. The panels were reduced in size to around 4 feet and were fixed along the lower part of the wall. The building was officially opened by the Earl of Onslow on 22nd October 1936. Co-incidentally, this was also the second day of the liquidator's sale in Southampton Docks of The Mauretania Syndicate items.

During the 1980s, because of fire regulations, the current occupants, Taunton's College, had the panels coated with some kind of fire retardant wax. Unfortunately, this caused problems with flaking and in November 2003, during renovations, they were removed and dispatched to France for reuse in a cottage.

MARQUIS OF GRANBY, BAMFORD

The Marquis of Granby was a hotel situated in the small village of Bamford, just west of Sheffield and on the edge of the Peak District National Park. Closed in 2002, the Marquis of Granby was well known for its interiors which came from White Star Line's *Olympic*, elder sister of *Titanic*. The hotel's owner before the Second World War was Harry Hutton who had travelled by sea and took a keen interest in ocean liners. *Olympic* was sold to the Sheffield-based shipbreakers Thomas W. Ward Ltd. for demolition at Jarrow-on-Tyne and in November 1935 her fixtures and fittings were auctioned by the London auctioneers Knight, Frank and Rutley. Interestingly, Thomas W. Ward lived at Endcliffe Vale House, not far from Bamford.

Harry Hutton purchased a quantity of *Olympic* fittings, including an Italian Renaissance-style bedroom, with its furniture and satinwood panelling. A number of other items were also installed in the hotel. However, some of the figured panels attributed to *Olympic* in the hotel's Olympic Bar are believed to have come from *Mauretania*. As it is known that Harry Hutton bought material from other ships, this would make sense although it is not possible to make a positive identification as the interiors of The Marquis of Granby have now been stripped and sold.

NONT SARAH'S, SCAMMONDEN

Some 23 miles to the north west of the Marquis of Granby is another country inn which is reputed to have *Mauretania* panels. The Nont Sarah's inn on Scammonden Moor near Huddersfield is 1,155 feet above sea level. Named after the founder's Aunt Sarah, sometime in the late 1930s the pub, with its nautical flavour, became one of the earliest themed inns in the area. The sun lounge overlooking the valley of Scammonden has rounded corners representing the bridge of an ocean liner and originally had a ships wheel. Without being able to examine the backs of the panels, it is difficult to determine where the wood fittings in Nont Sarah's came from on *Mauretania*. Some of the walnut figured panels appear to be from suites in first class.

Some of the walnut panels in the Nont Sarah's inn may have come from *Mauretania*.

OTHER ITEMS FROM MAURETANIA

This voyage of discovery has also uncovered other interesting *Mauretania*-related items. No doubt there are many more but below are listed a few in both the public and private domain.

Ship's wheel
The main ship's wheel was excluded from the May 1935 sale and its whereabouts is unknown. However, the steering wheel from the aft wheelhouse below the docking bridge (lot 3484) sold for £31.10.0d and was incorporated into the gate of a house at Audenshaw, Manchester. Unfortunately, the buyer's name is not clear in the catalogue and could be Bone or Bohn. It is possible that a Captain Barnes, who lived in the house for a number of years, could have been the gentleman who bought the wheel.

In 1996, the *Mauretania* wheel was sold in an auction for £4,500, and is now in private ownership.

Top: A poor image of the aft wheel in the gate of a house at Audenshaw. Bottom: The aft wheel is in a private collection.

Brass *Mauretania* letters
Although Walter Martin bought the 24-inch-high brass port and starboard *Mauretania* bow letters, only the port letters were included in The Mauretania Syndicate catalogue and these were subsequently sold in the liquidator's sale to a Plymouth buyer. They were acquired in the 1970s by the then tenant of The Mauretania bar and restaurant in Bristol. Incorporated into the Park Street building, they were later taken down and are now in storage. A letter E from the starboard side can be found in the Discovery Museum, Newcastle.

The same Plymouth buyer bought the 20-inch-high *Mauretania* Liverpool stern lettering. These ended up in the ownership of John Tinkler from Liverpool, who donated them to the Public Museums at Liverpool in 1940 and are now with the Merseyside Maritime Museum.

The first three letters of the port bow letters now in The Mauretania

Ship's bells
The only ship's bell offered for sale in the 1935 auction was the foremast crow's nest bell, which was bought by Harold Sandrey. This 20-inch-wide brass bell fetched 60 guineas and was featured in The Mauretania Syndicate catalogue. In 1974 the National Maritime Museum, Greenwich acquired the bell from a private collection and it is currently on display in the Passenger Gallery.

The crow's nest bell.

A slightly smaller, 18-inch-wide bell is in the Merseyside Maritime Museum. This uninscribed bell is similar to the one salved from the wreck of *Lusitania* in 1982, and possibly came from the stern docking bridge. It was presented in 1936 to Bebington Parish Church Council, Wirral by the then Chairman of Cunard White Star Line, Sir Percy Bates. Until the late 1970s it was used as the church bell in the Mission Church in Storeton Village. This is not far from the Cammell, Laird shipyard where the second *Mauretania* was built. The church gave the bell to Merseyside Maritime Museum in 1989.

The museum also owns a lifebuoy from *Mauretania*, a Red Ensign, and a pair of binoculars engraved with the ship's name which fetched five guineas in the 1935 sale.

Main whistle

Mauretania's main triple bell whistle on the forward funnel was bought by a Mr. Hanson for £52.10.0d and was removed from the ship on 13th June 1935. Controlled from the bridge, this electrically operated steam whistle consisted of three whistles of varying sizes. Around 1910 it replaced *Mauretania*'s original organ pipe whistle. Manufactured by Smith-Hyson, it is of the same type fitted to *Aquitania* and White Star Line's *Olympic*-class trio. Each whistle on these ships had its own unique and distinctive tone.

From the mid-1930s it was used at the British Thomson-Houston company at Rugby. The Rugby firm later became part of GEC, and in the early 1980s the whistle was bought by Roland Humble. Weighing around 9.75 cwts, the whistle is occasionally taken to steam fairs for a 'whistle blow'. It is on display in Mr. Humble's private Whistle Museum in Bodmin, Cornwall, along with the organ pipe whistle from *Aquitania*'s second funnel and whistles from the Isle of Man Steam Packet Co. Ltd.'s *King Orry* (2,485/1946) and *Snaefell* (2,489/1948).

In May 1988, another whistle from the British Thomson-Houston factory was given to the Southampton Maritime Museum on permanent loan. This is on display in the main entrance of the museum and, although it purports to be from *Mauretania*, it is in fact the factory whistle.

Discovery Museum, Newcastle

The Discovery Museum, Newcastle has probably one of the most impressive collections of objects from *Mauretania*. These include: an engine-room telegraph; port and starboard navigation lights; deep-sea lead; name plate from a capstan; jack-staff; engine room notice board; main engine manoeuvring wheel; revolution counter; turbine controls; oil pressure gauges; ship's plating; ship-builder and engine-builder name plates; lifebuoy; fog triangle and three links of the anchor chain. The engine-room telegraph was presented to Swan, Hunter and Wigham Richardson's chairman E.J. Hunter by Max Wilkinson, Managing Director of Metal Industries subsidiary, Shipbreaking Industries Ltd. Max Wilkinson appears on board *Mauretania* in the photographs taken before the 1935 sale on pages 74 and 75.

Also in the Discovery Museum is the recently renovated *Turbinia*, Charles Parson's record breaker, which started the marine turbine revolution in 1897.

Swan, Hunter and Wigham Richardson's detailed plans for *Mauretania* have been deposited at the Tyne and Wear Archives, Newcastle.

***Mauretania* models**

One of the contract specifications for the building of *Mauretania* was that the shipyard had to produce 'A fully-equipped model...handed over to the owners on the completion of the ship. The model to be rigged, fitted with all work in detail on the weather decks, and supplied in an air-tight glass case and table complete.'

One of the finest models of *Mauretania* can be found in the Discovery Museum. This 1: 48 scale builder's model is over 16 feet and was loaned to the then Tyne and Wear Museum in 1961 by Swan, Hunter and Wigham Richardson. The museum also has another fine 1: 48 scale model, on loan from Swan, Hunter, but not on display. This half model was once in the Science Museum, London and shows the hull plating.

Two similar size builder's models of *Mauretania* were made for Cunard Line. One is in the National Maritime Museum, Greenwich whilst the other resides across the Atlantic, in the Smithsonian Institution, Washington. The NMM model had originally been given by Cunard White Star Line to Winchester

Left: The main triple whistle being removed in June 1935. *[Southern Daily Echo]*
Right: The whistle is now in the Whistle Museum. Bodmin.

The model in the Discovery Museum, Newcastle.

Seen here in 1935, the Winchester Cathedral model is now in the National Maritime Museum.

Cathedral in 1935. It was officially unveiled in the Cathedral on 24th July 1935. Cunard White Star Line was represented at the ceremony by its one time chairman, Sir Thomas Royden, and the congregation consisted of many of *Mauretania*'s former officers and crew, including Captain Sir Arthur Rostron and Captain McNeil, commanders of the great liner. The Dean and Chapter of Winchester Cathedral sold the model to the National Maritime Museum in 1966.

The model in the Smithsonian shows *Mauretania* in her final guise as a cruise ship, painted white with green boot-topping, although her lifeboat configuration is as built. It was presented to President Franklin D. Roosevelt, a keen shipping enthusiast, by Bob Blake, head of Cunard Line in the United States. In 1932 the Science Museum, London returned to Cunard Line, at its request, a loan model of *Mauretania* which had been in the museum since 1925. In 1933 Roosevelt became President of the United States and *Mauretania* was painted white. It is more than likely that these two models are the same. In July 1935 President Roosevelt donated his maritime collection, including the model, to the Smithsonian Institution. Since then it has had a chequered career. Between 1972 and 1992 it was loaned for display aboard *Queen Mary* at Long Beach, California. It then underwent conservation work and was placed in storage, where it remains.

A fifth *Mauretania* model of the same dimensions is aboard the *Queen Elizabeth 2*. Situated opposite the entrance to the Caronia Restaurant on the Quarter Deck, this model is internally lit by fibre

The large *Mauretania* model on *Queen Elizabeth 2* is in fact *Lusitania*.

optic lights. It also has a specially designed backdrop based on an Atlantic chart. However, closer examination of the details of the bridge front and forward superstructure reveal that it in fact depicts her sister ship, *Lusitania*. This builder's model was in Cunard Line's Berkeley Street, London headquarters until 1994 when it became part of *Queen Elizabeth 2*s Cunard Heritage Trail, which offers a unique look at the 166-year history of this famous company. A smaller model of *Mauretania* can be found in the Mauretania Restaurant whilst in officers' mess on *Queen Elizabeth 2* is one of *Mauretania*'s engine room telegraphs which used to be on display in the former Mauretania Restaurant on *Queen Elizabeth 2*. There is also, on the Quarter Deck, an immense canvas painting, measuring over 8 by 6 feet, of the newly-completed *Mauretania* leaving the Tyne. This is by Thomas Hemy (1852-1937), younger brother of the Victorian painter, Charles Napier Hemy.

This small model is still on display aboard *Queen Elizabeth 2*. The engine room telegraph from the *Mauretania* is in the officer's mess.

Finally, in the Science Museum, London there is a fine, but smaller, although equally impressive 1: 64-scale model of *Mauretania*, measuring just over 12 feet. Since 1938 this has been on permanent loan to the museum from Swan, Hunter and Wigham Richardson. Another unusual loan item at the museum is a 1: 27 scale model of one of her four-bladed propellers. These replaced the three-bladed ones in 1909. The Manganese Bronze and Brass Co. Ltd. lent this item in 1937.

Close up of the Science Museum model.

Souvenir items

Before the Second World War teak decking from famous ships was used to produce small souvenir trinkets such as paper knives, miniature barrels and napkin rings. Those from *Mauretania* usually have a small metal label with the words: 'From the decking of the Mauretania. The old lady of the Atlantic'.

The Hughes Bolckow Shipbreaking Co. Ltd., shipbreakers based in Blyth, Northumberland, also specialised in making garden furniture from teak decking. They bought a large quantity of teak decking from *Mauretania* and produced a number of items including wooden chaise-longue chairs and a *Mauretania* garden seat with an outline of the ship and *'RMS Mauretania'* on the back rest. They were not cheap, priced at £5.5.0s and £6.15.0s respectively. The company also produced an attractive small mantle clock made from *Mauretania*'s teak.

Another interesting item appeared in 1939, when a medallion was made to celebrate the introduction of the new *Mauretania*. One side featured the new ship, and on the other was: 'This medallion is made from metal from the old Mauretania 1906-1935'.

Small original pieces of furniture also occasionally turn up for sale and during preparation for this book, a beautiful small maple cabinet from one of *Mauretania*'s first class suites was bought at a local charity auction in Dorset.

Thus, one hundred years after her birth, the legend of *Mauretania* lives on in the many pieces which once graced her magnificent interiors.

Miniature barrel made from *Mauretania's* teak decking.

This maple cabinet, made from two smaller cabinets, was bought at a Dorset charity auction. Note the detail of the handles and hinges and the brass stringing in the doors. This probably came from one of *Mauretania*'s first class suites.

R.M.S. MAURETANIA
A HAPPY ENDING FOR THE TIMBERS OF THE MAJESTIC VESSEL WHICH WAS THE PRIDE OF ALL ENGLAND
The "MAURETANIA" Chaise-Longue. Delightfully comfortable, and a really fine specimen of first class timber and workmanship. The whole chair folds up into a depth of about 7½" when not in use. Made from "Mauretania" Teak. £5 . 5 . 0.
THE "MAURETANIA" seat. A unique design with the outline of the vessel engraved on the back laths and its name on the lower back rail.
Price for the seat made from "Mauretania" Teak in 5ft. length, £6 . 15 . 0.
A piece of Garden Furniture made from the seasoned Teakwood of the well known Cunard Liner R.M.S. "MAURETANIA" will serve as an everlasting memento. We have purchased the whole of this Teakwood from the breakers, and are making specially designed Garden Furniture from it to mark the end of the vessel's life and keep alive its honoured memory. Every piece cabinet-made by skilled craftsmen. Other "MAURETANIA" designs shown in a special leaflet we have prepared. Write for free copy, together with complete catalogue of Garden Furniture, Gates, Doors, etc.
MAKERS OF THE WELL-KNOWN BATTLESHIP TEAKWOOD GARDEN FURNITURE
THE HUGHES BOLCKOW SHIPBREAKING CO. LTD. COLLINGWOOD WHARF, BLYTH NORTHUMBERLAND

Hughes Bolckow at Blyth, renowned for the manufacture of garden furniture from reclaimed timber, did not have sufficient teak to meet demand. Supplies had to be bought in from other ship-breakers and consequently the whole of *Mauretania's* teak was purchased followed shortly after by that from the *Leviathan.*

MAURETANIA HERITAGE TRAIL

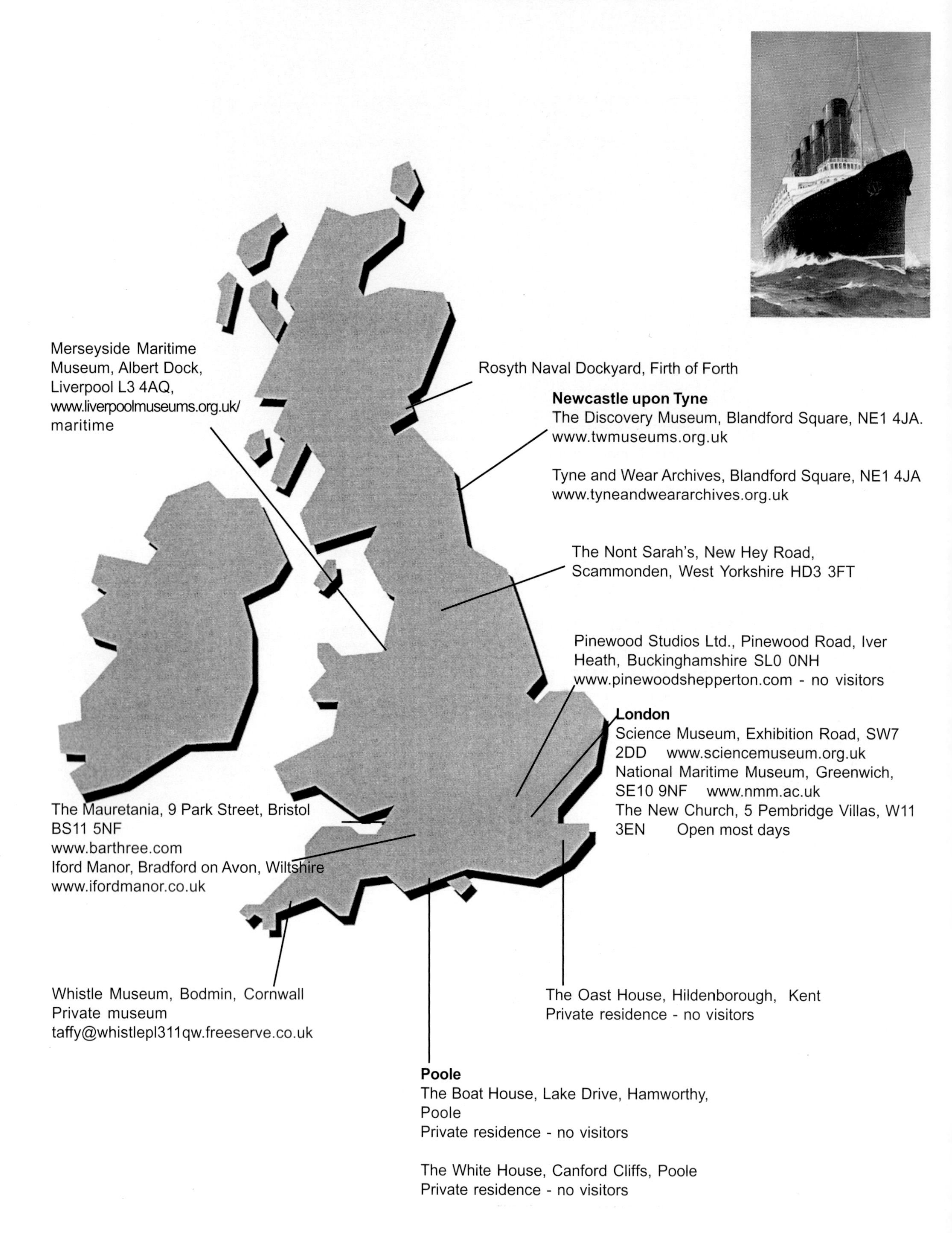

Merseyside Maritime Museum, Albert Dock, Liverpool L3 4AQ, www.liverpoolmuseums.org.uk/maritime
Rosyth Naval Dockyard, Firth of Forth
Newcastle upon Tyne
The Discovery Museum, Blandford Square, NE1 4JA. www.twmuseums.org.uk
Tyne and Wear Archives, Blandford Square, NE1 4JA www.tyneandweararchives.org.uk
The Nont Sarah's, New Hey Road, Scammonden, West Yorkshire HD3 3FT
Pinewood Studios Ltd., Pinewood Road, Iver Heath, Buckinghamshire SL0 0NH www.pinewoodshepperton.com - no visitors
London
Science Museum, Exhibition Road, SW7 2DD www.sciencemuseum.org.uk
National Maritime Museum, Greenwich, SE10 9NF www.nmm.ac.uk
The New Church, 5 Pembridge Villas, W11 3EN Open most days
The Mauretania, 9 Park Street, Bristol BS11 5NF
www.barthree.com
Iford Manor, Bradford on Avon, Wiltshire
www.ifordmanor.co.uk
Whistle Museum, Bodmin, Cornwall
Private museum
taffy@whistlepl311qw.freeserve.co.uk
The Oast House, Hildenborough, Kent
Private residence - no visitors
Poole
The Boat House, Lake Drive, Hamworthy, Poole
Private residence - no visitors
The White House, Canford Cliffs, Poole
Private residence - no visitors